Presented to

_____

By

_____

On the Occasion of

_____

Date

_____

ARMED FORCES
PRAYERS &
PROMISES

DEBRA SINDELDECKER
with contributors from the military community

BARBOUR
PUBLISHING

Published by Barbour Publishing, Inc., P.O. Box 719, Uhrichsville, Ohio 44683, www.barbourbooks.com

Our mission is to publish and distribute inspirational products offering exceptional value and biblical encouragement to the masses.

Member of the
Evangelical Christian
Publishers Association

Printed in the United States of America.
5 4 3 2 1

DEDICATION

This book is dedicated to. . .
those who selflessly serve their country
spouses who bear burdens alone
children missing a parent
concerned parents and family members
friends missing friends
and those who have lost loved ones.

I also dedicate the book to my husband,
Avionics Electronics Technician Chief Petty Officer
(AW/SW) Scott K. Sindeldecker, who is proudly
serving in the United States Navy.
Your twenty years of devoted military service have
inspired me to create this book for you and for all
who are affiliated with the armed forces.

A SPECIAL NOTE:

This book is a compilation of 180 prayers and promises, written by thirty people across the United States who have various connections to the armed forces. The writers are currently serving or are veterans of the armed forces, are spouses or other relatives of military service members, or are linked to the military through their communities. May your soul be blessed as you read the inspiring messages God has laid on each of their hearts.

———

*The prayer on page 41 was one of the prayers used the opening night of Operation Iraqi Freedom with marines from units of Marine Aircraft Group 39 stationed in Ali Al Salem, Kuwait.

*The prayer on page 183 was a prayer used on the flight line the opening night of Operation Iraqi Freedom with marines from Marine Aircraft Group 39 stationed in Ali Al Salem, Kuwait.

Contents

Loss of a Comrade

Let go of anger, and leave rage behind.
Do not be preoccupied. It only leads to evil.

Psalm 37:8 GW

Yes, Lord, I hear when You tell me to let go of my anger; but my enemies—Your enemies who reject mercy and justice—just killed my buddy! How can I rest when they have not received punishment?

However, Lord, You have told me that being consumed with repaying evil with evil only continues the cycle of hate, rage, and anger. Please forgive me for seeking revenge. Help me to be like Your Son, who forgave the anger and hatred of others.

From my perspective, the death of my friend is senseless and meaningless, which makes my blood boil. Yet, Father, when Your Son died from senseless brutality, Your blood flowed with love, offering me life and forgiveness. Remove my anger and make me more like You.

Thomas B. Webber

FIGHTING

*A hothead stirs up a fight,
but one who holds his temper calms disputes.*

PROVERBS 15:18 GW

God, it's so easy to get into a fight. Whenever I feel like someone has wronged me, I just want to strike back. This mood usually displays itself in physical violence. I know that when I act like this I am being irresponsible with my emotions instead of being rational.

As a leader of others, I must demonstrate a calm demeanor. I am reminded of a father and a son who showed the opposite approach to leadership. King Saul was a hot-tempered man who reacted to minor things and almost killed his son, Jonathan. However, Jonathan was calm in the face of chaos, bringing peace to the moment. His judgment was beneficial to those he led.

Father God, give me an attitude that responds, rather than reacts, to life's minor irritations. Create in me a calmness that brings peace when others try to start fights.

Thomas B. Webber

OVERCOMING ANGER

Better to get angry slowly than to be a hero.
Better to be even-tempered than to capture a city.

PROVERBS 16:32 GW

Lord, when people see us with our uniforms on, they see us as heroes—victors of the values we share. There are times when I do not feel like a hero. I am not a hero when I have treated a fellow human being with brutality or as a slave, making him serve my every want. On our uniforms we wear ribbons and medals that display our hero status; however, when we lose our tempers with our children, we are no longer their heroes.

God, I confess to You all the words I have said in anger toward my children and the impatience I have shown in their presence. Help me to be even-tempered and to be slow to get angry, because being a hero for my nation is nothing compared to being a hero to my family—especially my children. Assist me in being patient and filling my home with calmness.

Thomas B. Webber

FORGIVING ANGER

Get rid of your bitterness, hot tempers, anger, loud quarreling, cursing, and hatred. Be kind to each other, sympathetic, forgiving each other as God has forgiven you through Christ.

EPHESIANS 4:31–32 GW

All my life, Lord, I have been keenly aware of those things that create anger and hatred, and the things that just stir the emotional pot, leading to chaos. I must confess that I have been a partner to much of the chaos in others' lives, because I was (and occasionally still am) a person of anger. But I have found that anger is not part of Your nature. As a matter of fact, anger is released through forgiveness.

You call us to be people of compassion, sympathy, and forgiveness. We cannot practice these core values if we are holding grudges, starting fights, or being offensive to others. Therefore, God, I want to turn over a new leaf and be more like You. I want to forgive others' anger as You have forgiven mine. Hold me to this, God, because I want to please You.

Thomas B. Webber

CAST YOUR CARES

Never worry about anything.
But in every situation let God know what you
need in prayers and requests while giving thanks.
Then God's peace, which goes beyond anything
we can imagine, will guard your thoughts and
emotions through Christ Jesus.

PHILIPPIANS 4:6–7 GW

Father, thank You for caring so much about us that You don't want us to be burdened with worries. In prayer and communication we have access to You and an invitation to cast ours concerns, fears, and hopes on You.

You've instructed us in Your Word not only to ask but also to believe when we ask that You'll meet our needs according to Your will.

Lord, I praise You because You know what we need even before we ask. Your Spirit will provide comfort to our hearts that cannot be matched by anything on this earth. Your love and understanding will give us the assurance that can keep us in the peace that only You can provide.

Roger D. Horne

LIFE MORE ABUNDANT

*Cast all your anxiety on him
because he cares for you.*

1 PETER 5:7

I stand in awe of the love You have for us, Lord. You left heaven, walked this earth as a man, felt all the joys and pains that we do, and paid the ultimate price for us. You know about our worries and cares. It is Your desire to take those worries from us, so that we not only have life but *the abundant life* we read about in Your Word.

You offer us the opportunity to lay our cares at Your feet.

God, I ask for the courage to lay my anxieties at Your feet. I want to develop my faith in You as I walk with You daily. Bless me today with the joy that can come only from You.

Roger D. Horne

WHAT TO SAY

An anxious heart weighs a man down,
but a kind word cheers him up.

PROVERBS 12:25

Worries can drain a soul of happiness and leave it empty. Kind words from another can bring a spark of light into an otherwise dark day. As Your children, Lord, we should be ready to share a kind word with others to lift them.

Father, please lead me and give me the opportunity to share with others a word that may bring a smile to a worried face.

I thank You each day for the peace that You provide as promised in Your Word: "Peace I leave with you, my peace I give unto you: not as the world giveth, give I unto you" (John 14:27).

Roger D. Horne

WHO HAS CONTROL?

Therefore I tell you, do not worry about your life,
what you will eat or drink;
or about your body, what you will wear.
Is not life more important than food,
and the body more important than clothes?

MATTHEW 6:25

Have you ever looked back on an event in your life that you fretted over? Usually we find that our worries produce no positive solution. There are things that we should be concerned with to some degree; but, if we were honest with ourselves, the majority of us probably could afford to lose a worry or two.

Heavenly Father, I do worry about things that I cannot control. Please help me remember Your faithfulness and know that You are in control, which is why You instructed us to give our worries to You. I want to rest in the assurance that You will provide and leave the things I cannot control to the One who does all things well.

Roger D. Horne

OPPORTUNITIES

*Because of the service by which you have proved
yourselves, men will praise God for the obedience
that accompanies your confession of the gospel
of Christ, and for your generosity in sharing
with them and everyone else.*

2 CORINTHIANS 9:13

I pray for focus today, because it's so easy to get sidetracked. Satan wants us to fail. I want to concentrate on the plan You have for me while I'm serving my country. I know I can only envision what You have for me each day if I act upon Your Word.

As I hide Your Word in my heart, lead me away from falling into sin. Help my witness to be stellar and my actions to be consistent. I want those with whom I serve to see Jesus in my everyday life and witness Your love and compassion in my life. Give me opportunities to serve You each day.

Steve Nagle

PRAISE

*He has declared that he will set you in praise,
fame and honor high above all the nations he has
made and that you will be a people holy to
the LORD your God, as he promised.*

DEUTERONOMY 26:19

I want to please You today, Lord. Any honor or praise I may receive I offer back to You. Turn my heart from the desire for commendation letters and a chest full of medals. Keep me humble as I walk in Your truth. Make me holy today as I follow Your Word: "Create in me a clean heart. . .and renew a right spirit within me" (Psalm 51:10 KJV).

My prayer is that Your promises will fill me with hope and power so that I can bring honor to You. I want to obey You. Help me to not seek man's praise. May the words of my mouth and the meditations of my heart be acceptable in Your sight, O Lord, my strength and my Redeemer.

Steve Nagle

NO PRAISE

Let another praise you, and not your own mouth,
someone else, and not your own lips.

PROVERBS 27:2

I remember coming home from Vietnam. Those were difficult days. There were no organized homecoming celebrations—no parades or recognition. There were only sneers and stares. I fought a war only to return to find that I was the enemy!

I had volunteered my services to my country. I had served well. I received medals and letters of commendation. My country offered no thanks for the job I was asked to do. Only shame and embarrassment were bestowed on me. Praise came from no one.

I stuffed those memories into a footlocker for years. I suffered in silence. In my depression, however, I found strength in You. Thank You for Your support. My heavy heart is comforted by Your presence. You are the Healer of war wounds. Thank You for being there when no one else cared.

Steve Nagle

AFFIRMATION

*And a voice from heaven said, "This is my Son,
whom I love; with him I am well pleased."*

MATTHEW 3:17

Thanks for the affirmation I find in You. I do not need the praise of man. I know You give strength to meet each challenge. You remind me that I am Your child, and I cry to You, "Abba, Father." You are there for me. You lift my feet out of the slippery slime and set me on a firm rock. You give me strength every day. Your peace calms my tired heart. Your love forgives my sin. Your faithfulness reminds me of Your love.

You encourage me, and I rely on Your steadfastness. Thank You for Your support through difficult times. To hear Your voice say, "Well done, good and faithful servant," is all I live for. Grant that my service to You and my country be pleasing in Your sight, O Lord.

Steve Nagle

CHRISTLIKE

*Your attitude should be the same
as that of Christ Jesus.*

PHILIPPIANS 2:5

Lord, we need the attitude of Christ at all times, especially as soldiers. Help us put others first, as Jesus did.

Let us enjoy the times of bonding with our fellow soldiers—whether we are sharing a meal or just talking about our thoughts and dreams. Bless us as we travel together for a common purpose, whether on foot or by boat, as Jesus traveled, or in cars or planes. Enable us to set our faces toward the work You have given us, and keep us from wavering when the way is hard.

We pray for Your will to be done. We need Your help to complete the mission before us.

Thank You for the opportunity to serve our fellowman, our country, and You.

Rose Allen McCauley

NEW MINDS

Be made new in the attitude of your minds.

EPHESIANS 4:23

Thank You, Lord, for the pleasure new things bring us: new friends, new clothes, new growth in spring, a newborn babe.

Thank You that You are willing to change our hearts and minds and fill them anew with Your love if we will only ask You.

Thank You for Jesus, whose death on the cross for our sins washes us with His blood and makes us as clean and white as snow.

Thank You for Your Holy Spirit, who indwells us, changing us from the inside out and making us new creations.

Thank You for being a God of new beginnings. I want to start every new day by asking You to guide me and help me have the attitude of Christ.

Rose Allen McCauley

RIGHT CHOICES

Those who live according to the sinful nature
have their minds set on what that nature desires;
but those who live in accordance with the Spirit
have their minds set on what the Spirit desires.
The mind of sinful man is death, but the mind
controlled by the Spirit is life and peace.

ROMANS 8:5–6

Thank You, Lord, for giving us the free will to choose You. Help us make the right choices every day.

Give us hearts that listen to You and minds that block out the clutter of everyday noise, and tune our hearts to hear Your voice.

We thank You for Your Holy Word. As we read it each day, help us follow it as a map to guide us along the right paths.

Put within us a desire to be led by Your Spirit and His plans for our lives instead of being led by our sinful natures and selfish desires.

We choose life and peace instead of death. We choose You.

Rose Allen McCauley

Changed Lives

Therefore, since Christ suffered in his body, arm yourselves also with the same attitude, because he who has suffered in his body is done with sin. As a result, he does not live the rest of his earthly life for evil human desires, but rather for the will of God.

1 Peter 4:1–2

Lord, as I read these words by the apostle Peter, I'm reminded that he denied Jesus three times. This same Peter witnessed the empty tomb. He later saw Jesus' pierced hands and side. Seeing the risen Christ made a complete change in Peter's life.

Peter knew how Christ had suffered. He also knew for certain that Christ had been resurrected and conquered death and sin. Peter later suffered for Christ. We're told in Acts that he was imprisoned at least twice for preaching about Christ. Church historians tell us that Peter was crucified upside down.

Help us, Lord, as Peter did, to follow Your will the rest of our earthly lives. We want our lives to be changed by You.

Rose Allen McCauley

TRAINING

*Train a child in the way he should go,
and when he is old he will not turn from it.*

PROVERBS 22:6

Lord, You promised that however I trained my son, "when he is old he will not turn from it." Even he has said that I trained him to know You and love You and serve You, but he has chosen ways not pleasing to You.

I pray, dear God, for You to have mercy on my son. As he goes through the rigors of basic training, give him the success that comes by accomplishing all that is set before him. Give him quick understanding and a heart to obey what his commanding officers require of him. Help him develop the physical and mental stamina needed to complete his training with honors.

Most of all, please draw my son's heart to back to You.

Beth Ziarnik

BELIEVING

*Everyone who believes that Jesus is the Christ
is born of God, and everyone who loves
the father loves his child as well.*

1 JOHN 5:1

Beloved Lord, I received a letter from my son this morning. In it he told me how You touched his heart when he went to church on the base Saturday night. He said the service was "fantastic" and that lately he had been turning "more and more toward Jesus." He mentioned reading his Bible and praying to You. He said he has "decided to take charge of [his] life in the best way possible" by leaving the "fast and foolish life" he had led in the past and devoting himself to You. He also said that his time in military service helped him come to this decision.

Lord, please bless our armed services, and thank You for answering my prayer!

Beth Ziarnik

OBEYING AUTHORITY

*Children, obey your parents in the Lord,
for this is right.*

EPHESIANS 6:1

Father, obedience is the right way to go. Since our son was a small child, we have taught him to obey those in authority over him, but obedience has not always come easy to him. Now that he is serving You in the armed forces, I pray that he will obey those whose rank is greater than his. I pray that he will promptly do his very best at each task he's given to perform.

When a matter deeply troubles him, I ask You to give him the wisdom to know when to speak up with respect and when to remain silent. In all matters, please give him the grace to obey and trust You with the right outcome.

Beth Ziarnik

HERITAGE

*Sons are a heritage from the LORD,
children a reward from him.*

PSALM 127:3

Lord, Your Word says my son is a heritage from You. *You* gave him into my safekeeping. I feel so inadequate to the task, especially now, while he is serving overseas with his unit. I know so little of the real dangers he faces, the duties he is called to perform, the challenges he must meet. I know You are with him and pray that You will keep him alert to imminent danger. Please keep him at his best while performing his duties. Help him meet his challenges with courage and honor. Surround him with Your hedge of protection.

Lord, please guide me as I pray for and encourage him, mindful of this sacred trust You placed in my life.

Beth Ziarnik

Peace

Blessed are those who mourn,
for they will be comforted.

Matthew 5:4

Lord, I'm learning to turn to You when I lose friends. I miss them, but Your Word says that all who put their trust in You are with You now. I praise You for that and for Your comfort when I turn to You with my sorrow and need. I believe You understand how to help me, because You also knew grief when Your friend Lazarus died.

Almost as soon as I start mourning the buddies I've lost, Your presence becomes very real, Lord, as if You're telling me You understand.

Thank You, Jesus, for the peace You bring. Even when the whole world seems to be in turmoil, I know I can always count on You to help me when I sorrow.

Kay Cornelius

COMFORT

Yea, though I walk through the valley of the shadow of death, I will fear no evil: for thou art with me; thy rod and thy staff they comfort me.

PSALM 23:4 KJV

The valley of the shadow of death is as real to me today as it was to David. Everywhere I look, evil men are against me. Without Your presence, Lord, I'd be too afraid to do my job. I treasure this psalm because it reminds me that You are in charge. Because of that, evil will always be defeated.

Lord, just as David sees You as the Shepherd who cares for and comforts His flock, I know You care for me in the same way. Like the shepherd who calls his flock by name and keeps each safe from harm, You're always there with me in every situation.

I praise You for looking out for me—especially in my own darkest valleys.

Kay Cornelius

MERCY

Indeed, he was ill, and almost died.
But God had mercy on him, and not on him only
but also on me, to spare me sorrow upon sorrow.

PHILIPPIANS 2:27

Paul wrote the Philippians about a man he calls his brother and fellow soldier. Although this man was very ill, he had recovered. Lord, I praise You for Paul, a soldier for the gospel who boldly told others about Jesus everywhere he went. I thank You for all the letters Paul wrote and especially for this one that tells how God had mercy on Paul's friend and fellow soldier.

Lord, I understand when Paul says the loss of his friend would have caused him great sorrow. His words reassure me that You are merciful. I thank You for each of the times You have shown Your mercy, and I pray for continued mercy for my family, my fellow soldiers, and myself.

Kay Cornelius

DEATH'S DEFEAT

*For God so loved the world, that he gave his only
begotten Son, that whosoever believeth in him
should not perish, but have everlasting life.*

JOHN 3:16 KJV

Thank You, God, for this truth. I can't imagine
the love it must have taken to send Jesus, Your
only Son, from Your wonderful glory to live as the
Son of Man in a sinful world, then to die on the
cross for my sins. I shake my head in wonder even
as I rejoice in my salvation.

Lord, the way You chose to redeem me is beyond my weak human ability to understand, but I
praise You for it. Even when life seems dangerous
and uncertain, I know I have everlasting life, because I believe in Jesus, my Savior.

As I continue to praise You, help me share the
wonderful news of Jesus' love with every "whosoever" I meet.

Kay Cornelius

COMMITMENT AND DEDICATION

"But as for you, be strong and do not give up, for your work will be rewarded."

2 CHRONICLES 15:7

I confess that morale is getting low and I'm growing weary, Lord. Help me remember my commitment and the work that must be done. You've given us this task, the skill we need, and the physical strength to complete this campaign. Please don't let us veer to the left or the right as we work for the glory of God and the safety of our country.

Sometimes it would be easy to slack off just a little, but that is not Your way. You require dedication and our very best. I want my work to be something You can reward. I leave it up to You to decide what is sufficient, because the only reward I need is Your approval.

Mary Ann Hayhurst

STAYING THE COURSE

I have fought the good fight,
I have finished the race,
I have kept the faith.

2 TIMOTHY 4:7

This battle is over, Lord. You have helped me stay the course and have kept me safe. You watched over me when danger pursued. There were times when the battles seemed too intense; then I thought of Your faithfulness and how You finished Your battle for my soul, and I was able to press on.

I was young when I started this journey. Now I am an experienced and skilled soldier. You placed others in my path to teach and direct me, and now I must pass on the knowledge I possess to new recruits.

Thank You for helping me fulfill my commitment to my country but most of all to You.

Mary Ann Hayhurst

OBEYING AUTHORITY

When a man makes a vow to the LORD or takes an oath to obligate himself by a pledge, he must not break his word but must do everything he said.

NUMBERS 30:2

Help me to be a person faithful in my vows, Lord. Let me count the cost before I promise to do something. My father was the kind of man who could borrow money on a handshake. I want to be that kind of man—honorable and trustworthy—a man who can be counted on to live up to his word.

I took an oath to defend this country and, with Your help, I will. It is my desire to obey those You have placed over me in authority, but most of all, I want to obey You and Your commands.

I want my words to glorify You, Lord, and I want to keep my word to others. But, above all else, I want to keep my promises to You.

Mary Ann Hayhurst

DEPENDING ON EACH OTHER

Be devoted to one another in brotherly love.

ROMANS 12:10

Father, how can I say I love these people when we were strangers a short while ago? Our lives will now depend on one another. Where will I find the camaraderie to actually care for them and their safety?

I will find it in You. Because of the love You have so freely given to me, I will be able to reflect that love to others.

We will soon be in an unfamiliar place, removed from everything we have relied on in the past. Let us learn to be a loving fraternity and discover that we can depend on one another. I need them as badly as they need me. Help me to be a person they can trust.

Mary Ann Hayhurst

GOD'S WILL

He who heeds discipline shows the way to life,
but whoever ignores correction
leads others astray.

PROVERBS 10:17

Discipline is an important part of life, Lord. Though it is hard when I go through it, You use it to mold me to Your perfect will. Help me learn when I go through the rough times, so that I will not make the same mistakes again.

In Your Word You tell me that the world watches my life, and if I keep doing wrong others might do the same things. You told us to be lights in a dark world.

Thank You for giving us free will, but help me remember that the right decisions may not always be the easy ones. Your nudging and shaping teach me while I am here on earth so that someday, in heaven, I may be perfect like You.

Kristin Bliss

SIGN OF LOVE

*When we are judged by the Lord,
we are being disciplined so that we will not
be condemned with the world.*

1 CORINTHIANS 11:32

Thank You, God, for the promise of life with You eternally! I know that my human nature causes me to sin, and Your punishment is meant to free me of unacceptable behavior.

I can rejoice in knowing that You are making me more like You every time I go through a dark time. The Bible says we drive a nail in Your hand every time we sin. Forgive me for the wrongs I commit against You, and help me to be strong enough to resist temptations.

Thank You, Lord, that You care enough to point me in the right way. I can't wait to rejoice with You in heaven, where the cares of this world are forgotten.

Kristin Bliss

STRENGTHENED RESOLVE

For God did not give us a spirit of timidity,
but a spirit of power, of love and of self-discipline.

2 TIMOTHY 1:7

Keep me close to You, Lord, as I struggle to accept the discipline of this life of service to others. Fill me with Your strength and guide me in Your ways as I face dangerous tasks and physical challenges. Mold me into a person of high moral character, and strengthen my resolve during adversity.

Remind me that discipline breeds obedience and order, which in turn creates confidence in myself and in my fellow soldiers. Discipline, whether self-imposed or imposed on me, may save my life and the lives of others. Let my service be acceptable to You and a light to others.

Thank You, Father, for the gift of faith and confidence in Your strength and everlasting love.

Carol Umberger

PAIN FOR A PURPOSE

*No discipline seems pleasant at the time,
but painful. Later on, however, it produces
a harvest of righteousness and peace for
those who have been trained by it.*

HEBREWS 12:11

O Lord, my heart is filled with questions today. I am facing a difficult situation. I don't like the anger and fear that are tearing me up on the inside. I feel misused and abused. The desire to lash out in self-defense nearly overwhelms me. But You have promised to be with me through all things and give me strength to endure the pain. You are my loving heavenly Father.

I accept this struggle as a discipline that You have allowed in my life to make me stronger in my trust and dependence on You. Please lead me step by step. Direct my thoughts and emotions. Lead me to the joy and peace that come only from trust and obedience to Your perfect will.

Wanda M. Royer

GOOD RELATIONSHIPS

Let us not give up meeting together, as some are in the habit of doing, but let us encourage one another —and all the more as you see the Day approaching.

HEBREWS 10:25

Father, as we gather in this tent on the eve of Operation Iraqi Freedom, we understand better than ever how important we, the body of Christ, are to each other. Our faith traditions matter little; our relationship with Your Son, Jesus, and with each other matters the most. Through our relationships, we minister to others and are ministered to. You created us to be in relationships, and we thank You for them.

As each new day approaches, and in the challenges that are ahead, prepare us through Your Word and Your presence, which we experience in the relationships we enjoy in this fellowship. We look to You with confidence because we have been encouraged by one another. We pledge to meet again as soon as possible upon returning from this evening's mission. Protect and provide for these marines.

Jim Ellis

A Godly Example

*"In everything I did, I showed you that
by this kind of hard work we must help the weak,
remembering the words the Lord Jesus himself said:
'It is more blessed to give than to receive.' "*

Acts 20:35

Jesus led by example, and this passage from Your Word, Lord, encourages us to do the same. It is easy to become self-absorbed and concerned only about my own needs, forgetting the needs of others. Help me to fix my eyes on Jesus, Father, so I might continually be reminded of His desire and Yours—for me to serve others. All that I have is Yours, Lord. I want to be ready to give to others as You have given to me.

Thank You for the talents and abilities You have given me. May I use them for Your honor and glory. I want to be ready to give an answer for the hope that is within me, so prepare me daily, Lord, to share with others.

Jim Ellis

PRAYER FOR LEADERS

He appointed military officers over the people and assembled them before him in the square at the city gate and encouraged them with these words: "Be strong and courageous. Do not be afraid or discouraged because of the king of Assyria and the vast army with him, for there is a greater power with us than with him."

2 CHRONICLES 32:6–7

The heavens and the earth speak of Your power, Lord. If we look to our left or to our right or to the heavens, we see Your mighty power in creation. You have appointed men of honor to lead our nation and armed forces. I pray that You will grant them wisdom and ability as they make decisions that affect so many.

No matter who the adversary is, I will not be discouraged, because there is no greater power than You, Lord. I have read of Your provision in the past, and I pray with confidence for provision and protection for those deployed and for their families at home. I will not be afraid. I will not be discouraged.

Jim Ellis

Maturing Trials

Consider it pure joy, my brothers, whenever you face trials of many kinds, because you know that the testing of your faith develops perseverance. Perseverance must finish its work so that you may be mature and complete, not lacking anything.

James 1:2–4

Lord, You want me to consider it pure joy when I and those I care for face trials? Forgive me for my lack of faith. Give me the perspective to see Your purpose in times of trial. I depend on the Holy Spirit to remind me that these trials are part of the perfecting and refining process You use to develop my faith so that I may be mature and complete—able to help others.

Help me accept Your testing with the knowledge that it is only because You love me. It is because You love me that You want me to mature. It is because You love me that You will never leave me nor forsake me, as we walk together through the trials of life.

Jim Ellis

PRAY FOR THEM?

*I tell you: Love your enemies and pray for
those who persecute you, that you may be sons
of your Father in heaven. He causes his sun to rise
on the evil and the good, and sends rain on
the righteous and the unrighteous.*

MATTHEW 5:44–45

God, my enemies need my prayers, even though
I have yet to pray for them. I do not want to pray
for them. They are evil men who are out to hurt
my family, but would it be fair to condemn them
to death when even You offer them life?

Who am I to determine that they need to die
when You hold even my life in the balance? I do
not have the heart to send anyone to hell, because
I know You are more merciful than that.

Bless my enemies, for they need Your grace
and mercy just like I do. Allow them to experience
the grace and mercy that You have shown me.

Amy S. Huehl

I DON'T LIKE THEM

I pursued my enemies and overtook them;
I did not turn back till they were destroyed.

PSALM 18:37

Lord, I thank You that You have given me the strength to overcome anything that comes into my path. There are some people in my life whom I just plain do not like. I know that even if I don't like them, they are people You have placed in my life for a reason.

Remind me that You keep me in Your care and that, no matter what happens, my enemies will not last long. In Your grace, You will allow me to triumph in their eyes, and they will be destroyed by You and You only.

You are my strength in the face of my enemies and will allow me to prevail in their sight. Thank You for being my victory.

Amy S. Huehl

WISDOM

*Your commands make me wiser than my enemies,
for they are ever with me.*

PSALM 119:98

Without Your Word, I would be ignorant. I know that it is only with the wisdom that You give me that I am able to overcome any situation in my life. I pray that You will show me what You want me to do in every situation and, in particular, the one that I am now facing.

Grant me Your wisdom. Show me Your mercy. Allow me to be wise in Your eyes.

I don't want to dwell on what my enemies are telling me is the truth. Instead, I want my mind to be focused on the truth I find in Your Word.

Amy S. Huehl

Protection

*For the LORD your God moves about in
your camp to protect you and to deliver your
enemies to you. Your camp must be holy,
so that he will not see among you anything
indecent and turn away from you.*

DEUTERONOMY 23:14

I praise You for living in my home and protecting my children and me and for protecting my loved ones when I am not able to be with them. You protect my family from all the attacks of the enemy. I praise You that You surround us with Your protection in a way that is beyond my human comprehension.

I am thankful that all Your ways are holy and that, in Your holiness, You have decided to call my family Your own. Thank You for allowing protection that I cannot see with my eyes but that I can feel in my spirit. It brings me peace.

Amy S. Huehl

DOUBT

*Now faith is being sure of what we hope for
and certain of what we do not see.*

HEBREWS 11:1

Lord, no one but You knows what tomorrow will bring. Though I can't see You, I can feel Your presence as I pray. How awesome You are to care for my concerns in such a personal way that I am invited to talk with You at will. I am amazed and astounded by Your greatness and Your compassion for me.

Keep me near You, so that we may walk closely together. Sometimes I question my circumstances, but I never doubt You. Help me show others who You are and that You are worthy of their faith.

Thank You for Your love, which is all that my hope and faith encompass.

Tamela Hancock Murray

Impossible Situations

He replied, "Because you have so little faith.
I tell you the truth, if you have faith as little as
a mustard seed, you can say to this mountain,
'Move from here to there' and it will move.
Nothing will be impossible for you."

Matthew 17:20

Sometimes my situation seems impossible. I am afraid, and I feel a loss of control. But when I turn to You, my faith in Your power to overcome all obstacles keeps me strong.

When You took the burden of my sin on the cross, You showed me that no hurdle is too great for You. Not a day goes by that I don't remember what You did for me. I am awed by Your attitude of complete submission and Your love for me.

Lord, thank You for the gift of faith and for giving me the knowledge that nothing is impossible with Your help.

Tamela Hancock Murray

BELIEVING WITHOUT SEEING

We live by faith, not by sight.

2 CORINTHIANS 5:7

Lord, at times I wish I could see You. To hear Your voice. . .to clasp Your hand. . . What a great comfort that would be! Your disciple, Thomas, had to put his hands in Your wounds before he would believe that You had risen. Help me to be among those who are blessed to have faith that does not need such proof.

The world around me sometimes makes fun of people who believe in someone they cannot see. Help me to be Your hands, feet, and mouth so that they can see You in me.

Thank You for a strong mind and body so that I can serve You where I am.

Tamela Hancock Murray

FAITHFUL LIVING

Let love and faithfulness never leave you;
bind them around your neck,
write them on the tablet of your heart.

PROVERBS 3:3

Lord, lead me through each day so that I will always follow Your moral compass, not someone else's. When You test me, guide me to the right decision so that I may be an example of love to others. You instructed us to forgive those who wrong us—not seven times but seventy-seven. Give me the patience to forgive others and the faithfulness to live in such a way that I will not offend others.

With words of wisdom from Your tender and gracious heart, You showed us how to live a pure life. Help me keep a pure heart, so that my words and actions will mirror Your love to the world.

Wrap me in the whole armor of love and faithfulness today. Sustain me, Lord.

Tamela Hancock Murray

PRECIOUS SACRIFICE

The LORD is my strength and my shield;
my heart trusts in him,
and I am helped.

PSALM 27:8

Thank You, Lord, for giving me strength to be the sole caregiver while my husband is away. Stepping in for him is very hard at times. The time and energy I use to care for my family is nothing compared to what You sacrificed for me.

Thank You, Lord, for our children. They are so very precious and special to us. My husband has missed much of their growing up, yet he is able to maintain a close relationship with them. I am thankful that our children understand why their dad must be away from home so much, and that they respect the duty he is called to serve.

Thank You, Lord, for being the anchor of our household.

Debra Sindeldecker

FOLLOW THE LEADER

Still another said, "I will follow you, Lord; but first let me go back and say good bye to my family."

LUKE 9:61

Lord, when I am called to duty far from home, give my family and me comfort in knowing You are with us. Saying good-bye is so difficult for all of us. Give us strength and understanding to endure this separation. Each time we have to say good-bye, it gets more and more difficult. Leaving is the hardest part. Through tears of sorrow, make the good-byes as comforting as possible.

Show me the path You have for me as I serve my country from so many miles away. Protect my family back home as I follow Your will for me. Keep them safe and let them know I love them, even though I am not there to show it.

Debra Sindeldecker

GIVE GENEROUSLY

He and all his family were devout and God-fearing; he gave generously to those in need and prayed to God regularly.

ACTS 10:2

Father, my family and I are so dedicated to You. Everything we have is Yours. Even though we know You and love You, we still fear You. Our fears make us stronger as we do our best to live for You. Let us not be self-centered. Lead us in all we do.

Guide me to give generously to those in need. I know You hear my every prayer. I see answers everywhere. You have shown me through prayer that You are with me wherever I go.

I have the privilege of meeting so many people over this great land. Keep me from passing up even one opportunity to share You with others. Teach me to be a giver of Your Word.

Debra Sindeldecker

TRUST AND OBEY

He must manage his own family well and see that his children obey him with proper respect.

1 TIMOTHY 3:4

God, help me to take care of my family as Your Word commands. Remind me to keep the duties for my family and the duties of my job separate, even though my military service makes it so difficult sometimes.

My family means so much to me. Help me to teach my children to trust me, as there is so much doubt in the world today. Help me to instill in my children a respect for me and for others.

Give me patience when stress overcomes me. Show my family I love them and support them, even though I may not always be there for them. Help me to manage my home and finances in a way that is pleasing to You, no matter where I am.

Debra Sindeldecker

IN BATTLE

*Though an army besiege me, my heart will not
fear; though war break out against me,
even then will I be confident.*

PSALM 27:3

Dear Lord, I pray for safety and strength for all those in battle. I pray for them to put their trust in You.

I thank You for always being with us and for being our shield and defender. I thank You for Your presence and power in whatever kinds of battles we may find ourselves—battles from without and those from within.

I thank You for victory in Jesus, who by His resurrection conquered death forever.

Deliver us from evil and the fear of evil, because we know that You are far greater. Give us the faith to conquer kingdoms in Your holy name.

Rose Allen McCauley

EMMANUEL—GOD WITH US

"Do not be afraid of them; the LORD your God himself will fight for you."

DEUTERONOMY 3:22

Dear Lord, just as Moses strengthened Joshua for battle by telling him that God would fight for him, help us to find strength in our daily battles—both physical and spiritual—from Your presence.

Help us to put on Your armor: the belt of truth; the breastplate of righteousness; the gospel of peace; the shield of faith; the helmet of salvation; and the sword of the Spirit, which is Your Word (Ephesians 6:14–17).

Lord, I want to stay *in* Your Word and stand *on* Your Word and its promises. Help us to feel Your presence and Your power and not to fear.

Rose Allen McCauley

GOD'S PROTECTION

*He shall say: "Hear, O Israel, today you are going
into battle against your enemies. Do not be
fainthearted or afraid; do not be terrified
or give way to panic before them."*

DEUTERONOMY 20:3

Lord, our natural tendencies of self-preservation would have us fear battle and go into a panic. I pray instead for Your peace that passes all understanding, even peace in the midst of battle.

Please give us clear minds, steady hands, and hearts set on You. Make us keenly alert to everything about us as we utilize the senses You have blessed us with: sight, hearing, touch, smell, and taste.

I thank You for the enjoyment these senses bring every day and for the protection they provide when in battle. Help us use them wisely for our own safety and the safety of our fellow soldiers. I thank You and praise You for all Your gifts, especially the gift of Your Son.

Rose Allen McCauley

TRUSTING GOD

He will have no fear of bad news;
his heart is steadfast, trusting in the LORD.

PSALM 112:7

Lord, it seems like the majority of the news media reports only bad news. It is so easy to get discouraged, disillusioned, and depressed when we dwell on those reports.

Help us instead to trust in You and keep our eyes and hearts steadfast on You.

We believe You have the whole world in Your hands. We know You feed the birds of the field, and we trust You to meet all our needs. Help us not to worry about today or tomorrow but seek Your kingdom and Your righteousness (Matthew 6:33–34).

We trust You whether the news seems good or bad, because You can work good out of bad. We know You are the God of miracles!

Rose Allen McCauley

LOVE

"Greater love hath no man than this,
that a man lay down his life for his friends."

JOHN 15:13 KJV

God, I pray not for myself but for the safety of all those with whom I serve. I want nothing more than to ensure that all of us will have a chance to see our families again. I love the United States and all it stands for, and I want to give it all I can give.

I found friends in the people with whom I serve, and I would, without a thought in my mind, take their places if they were in danger. God, help me to live up to that thought.

I love You, God, and want nothing more than to do my best in all I do. I know that is possible with Your help.

Roberto Miguel Cerda

THE LORD

*The LORD thy God, he will go over before thee,
and he will destroy these nations from before
thee, and thou shalt possess them.*

DEUTERONOMY 31:3 KJV

Jesus, You are the Lord of my life. As I sit here, serving my country, I think of all the things I am missing, and I wonder if I made the right choice. Then I think of all You gave for me and wonder if I am doing enough.

Jesus, You are the most important thing in my life. As I sit here, facing the possibility of death, I am not afraid, for You are with me. You will help me in all that I do to possess the enemy that comes against me.

Jesus, help me to be like You—to lay down what I have for You.

Roberto Miguel Cerda

STRENGTH

The LORD is my strength my song;
he has become my salvation.

EXODUS 15:2

God, give me strength to deal with all that is around me. I want so much to do my best and to be the man You want me to be. It is hard to do that with all the shooting and the death around me.

I love You, Jesus, and I want to leave here and serve You in the way that I want to. But then I remember that You have put me here, and You have a plan for my life. I look forward to what is in store for me.

Jesus, take my life and use it for Your will.

Roberto Miguel Cerda

HONOR

Ye shall do no unrighteousness in judgment:
thou shalt not respect the person of the poor,
nor honour the person of the mighty.

LEVITICUS 19:15 KJV

God, You have put me here in harm's way, and I don't understand why. You have put me where I could possibly lose my life and never see my mother and my family again.

But I will do my best for You, because You have done Your best for me. There is no place I would rather be than where You have sent me. If I were to lose my life here in this country far from my home, You would be there with me.

I remember You were there for me when I was not there for You. Thank You, Jesus.

Roberto Miguel Cerda

FREE TO WORSHIP

*Live as free men, but do not use your freedom
as a cover-up for evil; live as servants of God.*

1 PETER 2:16

Lord, I praise You that I live in a free country—free to worship You openly. Yet, many Christians in our schools and public places are restricted from praying in Your name.

Our men and women in military service have died to keep our land free. I pray that all of Christ's followers in America will be legally set free to worship You in every public place.

I pray that Christians may remain free to live as servants of God, so that those who died for our freedom will not have died in vain.

I pray that we will not misuse the freedom we have in Christ or become complacent but that we will be willing to give our all—if it is required—to retain our freedom of worship.

Anne Greene

FREE TO WALK

I will walk about in freedom,
for I have sought out your precepts.

PSALM 119:45

Lord, I thank You for our men and women in military service who gave Americans the right to walk this great land in freedom. Even more, I thank You for Christ's life, death, and resurrection. These made available the free gifts of victorious and abundant living and eternal life.

Lord, I thank You for the freedom to walk in Jesus' way, in His Word, and in His teaching. I thank You that I will be secure as I walk the lifestyle given by Your precepts.

Lord, I thank You for the freedom to seek You with all my heart, the freedom to communicate You with my lips, and the freedom to follow You. Don't let me forget how much my freedom cost.

Anne Greene

FREE TO WITNESS

*Now the Lord is the Spirit, and where the Spirit
of the Lord is, there is freedom.*

2 CORINTHIANS 3:17

Lord, even in countries that are not free, as America is free, Your Spirit shines the light of the knowledge of God in the darkness of men's hearts. You are calling men and women from oppressed countries all over the world to seek freedom in America. You are calling Muslims, Buddhists, Hindus—people from all religions—to our free country so that we, as Christ's followers, might tell those living in bondage and darkness about the freedom that comes with knowing Christ.

Show us how to become bold soldiers for Christ: filled with love, filled with His Spirit, not counting the cost, and sharing our good news of the gospel with those who are seeking freedom.

Help us use our freedom to be Your witnesses to those who are living in bondage.

Anne Greene

FREE TO FIGHT

Recently you repented and did what is right in my sight: Each of you proclaimed freedom to his countrymen. You even made a covenant before me in the house that bears my Name.

JEREMIAH 34:15

Lord, I pray that America will not be as Israel was in Jeremiah's day. The Israelites repented and did right in Your sight, even making a covenant before You in the temple. But they changed their minds and disobeyed You again. So, You sold Israel into slavery to the Babylonians.

Lord, may we, as Christ's followers in America, not change our minds and wills from following You! Instead, help us be conformed to Your image and Your will, so that You will keep our country free. We want to be soldiers of Christ, wearing God's full armor and fighting the good fight until You come.

I pray that we will be found faithful unto death, soldiers of the cross. Lord, keep our country free.

Anne Greene

MY ALLEGIANCE TO GOD AND COUNTRY

Show me your ways, O LORD, teach me
your paths; guide me in your truth and teach me,
for you are my God my Savior,
and my hope is in you all day long.

PSALM 25:4–5

Dear Lord, You know my heart, my innermost desires, and my feelings. I love You—the Savior of my life. I want my whole life to be pleasing to You.

But, Lord, You understand how I so often feel that I am owned by others who control my thoughts, my actions, my responsibilities, and my goals. It is tough to be obedient to my job, my life commitments, and still feel I am being faithful to Your teachings.

Please show me, Lord, how to display Christ-like behavior and attitudes as I face the ungodly world in which I live and work. My hope and trust are in You, my heavenly Father.

Wanda M. Royer

GOD IS WITH ME ALWAYS

For this God is our God for ever and ever;
he will be our guide even to the end.

PSALM 48:14

O Lord, how my heart swells with praise and gratitude when I think of who You are. You are mighty and wise beyond all I can imagine or comprehend. Even though You are over, under, and around all of life and matter, You still love and care about insignificant, little me. I am humbled. I stand in awe of You.

The Bible is filled with Your promises to be with me, to strengthen and guide me, and to take me at the end of my life to be with You forever and ever. I am filled with peace and joy.

I will remain faithful to You. I will entrust my life daily into Your hands. Keep me strong and make me aware of Your presence wherever I am.

Wanda M. Royer

REWARDS FROM
FOLLOWING GOD

You guide me with your counsel,
and afterward you will take me into glory.

PSALM 73:24

O Lord, Your Word reminds me that all the riches of the world and all the praise and recognition of people do not bring lasting joy and peace. Nothing compares to the assurance and peace I feel when I sense Your approval on my life after I have asked for Your counsel and wisdom and then lived by it.

Heaven begins in my heart as I commune with You. I look forward with joy and anticipation to the time when You will receive me into Your glorious eternal home in heaven.

All praise to You, my God and Redeemer.

Wanda M. Royer

WISDOM FOR TODAY

*I guide you in the way of wisdom
and lead you along straight paths.*

PROVERBS 4:11

O God of all creation, I acknowledge that You know all about me: the thoughts in my mind, the desires of my heart, and the turmoil in my emotions. Your wisdom is truth. You sent Your Holy Spirit to live within me, to lead me in the understanding of Your wisdom, and to teach me Your will.

You gave me the Bible to show me how to live by Your plan. I ask You to lead me to the scripture verses that will open my understanding and reveal Your answers for my need today.

Speak to my heart as I sit in quietness before You right now. I love You. I need You. I am Yours. Please bless me with Your peace and understanding.

Wanda M. Royer

GOD'S WORD IS MEDICINE

*Dear friend, I pray that you may enjoy good
health and that all may go well with you,
even as your soul is getting well.*

3 JOHN 1:2

I thank God every day for those who volunteer to
protect our country, to make it a safer place to live.
I pray they will stay in good health and that all will
go well while they are so far from home. I pray that
their families are safe and healthy. I pray they will
meditate on God's Word, as it will strengthen them
and will direct their paths. God's Word is medicine
to our souls and strength to our bodies.

How wonderful it is, Lord, that You want the
best for me. Thank You for providing me with a
sound mind and good health. Thank You that I
can rest, knowing that You are watching over my
family, too.

Flavia Crowner

A JOYFUL HEART

A cheerful look brings joy to the heart,
and good news gives health to the bones.

PROVERBS 15:30

I'm thankful, Lord, that You have blessed me with a family. They pray daily for my well-being while I'm away on foreign soil defending our country. They bless me with letters, family photos, and care packages filled with my favorite items.

It brings joy to my soul when I see the faces of my loved ones and read their letters of encouragement and family news. But the greatest blessing of all is knowing I'm in the family of God—that You promised me everlasting life and a home with You.

Lord, I am amazed how much You love me and bless me. I pray that my love for You will bring others into a saving knowledge of Jesus Christ.

Flavia Crowner

MEDITATING ON HIS WORD

*For physical training is of value, but godliness
has value for all things, holding promise for
both the present life and the life to come.*

1 TIMOTHY 4:8

While in the military service, I attended boot camp to be physically fit to service our country. But it didn't prepare me for living a godly life. Therefore, I studied the Bible like a soldier arming myself with God's Word for battle.

I learned that the joy of You, Lord, is my strength and that You will give me the desires of my heart. I'm instructed to rejoice and be glad in all matters. Meditating on Your Word day and night has given me confidence in my everyday living, and it holds the promise of one day being with You.

Thank You, Lord, for the blessings You have for us through godly living—blessings both here on earth and throughout eternity.

Flavia Crowner

LONG LIFE

"Say to him, 'Long life to you!
Good health to you and your household!
And good health to all that is yours.' "

1 SAMUEL 25:6

I praise You, God, that You care for Your people. You want us to have long life and be in good health so that we can enjoy the good things You have provided for us: the joy of families and friends, the privilege of living in a country in which we have the freedom to worship You. We can reside in a country that provides military forces to defend and to preserve our freedom so that families can live in peace and in good health.

How great it is that we are blessed with long life and good health—to enjoy the things You have given us here on this earth. But what greater reward it will be when we go home to live with You.

Flavia Crowner

HOME AND FAMILY

When his time of service was completed,
he returned home.

LUKE 1:23

Thank You, Lord. You have kept me safe during my time away from home. You have set guardian angels around my family and kept them safe. Soon we will be reunited.

Without Your love and strength, my journey would have been impossible; my prayers would have gone unheard. Without Your presence, my family would have felt fearfulness and loneliness. Instead, they felt bold and happy to be a part of the great family of believers around them.

I praise Your name, Father, and thank You for my home and my family. I want to be a blessing to others and always live according to Your will.

Bettye Powell Glydewell

SHARING

Jesus did not let him, but said,
"Go home to your family and tell them
how much the Lord has done for you,
and how he has had mercy on you."

MARK 5:19

Thank You, Father, for the opportunity to share what You have done for us. Thank You for the compassion You have shown to us when we have been ill or sad or weary. Without You, Lord, there would be no hope.

Please help me to lead my life so that unbelievers will see You in me and want to know You as their Savior. Help me to lead my life so that believers will be strengthened and emboldened to share the Good News. I sing Your praises, Lord.

Bettye Powell Glydewell

Faithfulness

*"My husband is not at home;
he has gone on a long journey."*

Proverbs 7:19

Precious Lord, I love You and I adore You.

I thank You, Lord, for giving me a loving and faithful spouse. We have built our home and marriage on our faith in You. Thank You for making us both strong. Each time we are apart, You have been faithful to "lead us not into temptation, but deliver us from evil." You have led us to make our marriage vows a top priority, and the rewards You have given us are many.

Please remind us daily of our love for each other.

Bettye Powell Glydewell

ACKNOWLEDGMENT

As you enter the home, give it your greeting.

MATTHEW 10:12

I acknowledge, Lord, that You are the head of our home and that You created the original home with Adam and Eve.

Help me always to be mindful that a home is so much more than just a house. It is the base that keeps us focused on You. It is the place we return to when we need to be refueled, when we need a hug or total acceptance.

I am in awe that You would love me enough to bless me with such a home. Help me, Father, to always glorify You in the way I choose to live— whether at home or away.

You have blessed us mightily, Lord; and I love, praise, and adore You for Your blessings.

Bettye Powell Glydewell

COMMITMENT

*"Those who honor themselves will be humbled,
but people who humble themselves
will be honored."*

LUKE 14:11 GW

Father, teach me to be committed to You, to uphold Your mighty Word. I want to be a good soldier in Your army. I know I can never do enough to gain Your favor. It is by grace You allow me near the throne.

Keep my heart humble and lowly. Jesus taught that we need to be servants, and I cannot serve with a heart full of pride. Show me the way You want me to serve. Thank You for Your mercy. Thank You for the opportunity to share Good News with those around me.

Remind me, Lord, who is in charge. Draw me near to You. Keep my footsteps on the right path, as I choose service to the King.

Eileen Key

Self-Assessment

He who ignores discipline comes to poverty and shame, but whoever heeds correction is honored.

Proverbs 13:18

Father, in Your Word You tell us You will create in us a clean heart. I ask for Your cleansing now. I want to be a person of honor, after Your own heart as King David was. In a gentle manner, Lord, would You clean the closets of my heart? Sweep out the dirt, and allow light to shine in. Wipe away the tears, fears, and doubts, Lord. Make me fresh and new.

I trust You with my life. I know You want the best for me. I bow to Your discipline that I might claim the scripture and be one of honor. I am blessed to be in the presence of the Almighty. Thank You, Lord, for Your promises.

Eileen Key

SHELTER FROM THE STORMS

My salvation and my honor depend on God;
he is my mighty rock, my refuge.

PSALM 62:7

O Lord, many times I want to cover my head with my own hands and know I am safe. Foolish me. Safety comes only in knowing You. Whether it is enemy artillery fire or angry words, You are my refuge.

Lord, help me understand that I need to call on You immediately and rush to Your side. Show me Your mighty works. Protect me, Father. Keep me safe, resting against the Rock.

I am learning it is not easy to walk this journey, and I grow tired in my own strength. Give me Your rest. Comfort me when I can no longer carry on. Draw me close to You. Allow my spirit to hear what You would say. Thank You, Lord.

Eileen Key

A WORTHY LEADER

*He was doubly honored above the Three
and became their commander, even though
he was not included among them.*

1 CHRONICLES 11:21

Make me worthy to be a leader. Whether it is a leader of one or of many, I cannot lead in my own strength. Jesus, You taught that to be first is to be last. Keep me last and lowly, dear Lord, for I am full of faults and sins. Don't let pride and vanity puff me up. Keep my focus on the cross.

I praise You, Father, for the chance to serve. I choose today to serve You and my fellowman. Open my ears and my eyes so I might see the needs around me. Show me the areas of weakness I need to bridge and build up. Teach me to be a commander in the army of God.

Eileen Key

WHAT IN THE WORLD IS GOING ON?

We were saved with this hope in mind.
If we hope for something we already see, it's not
really hope. Who hopes for what can be seen?
But if we hope for what we don't see,
we eagerly wait for it with perseverance.

ROMANS 8:24–25 GW

Why am I here? Why did You let this happen? An ocean, a world, and a conflict separate me from my family. I can only remember their faces and hold them in my heart. Help me grab onto the hope that time will pass, that You will fulfill Your purpose for me here, and that one day I'll see them again.

What was it like when You were assigned to earth and away from heaven? Did the hope of a reunion with Your Father keep You going? The price I pay is small compared to the price You paid. I can't see the end of this tour, but I know You do. Thanks for keeping hope alive in me and helping me to persevere.

Lynette Sowell

WHO'S IN CHARGE HERE?

May God, the source of hope, fill you with
joy and peace through your faith in him.
Then you will overflow with hope by
the power of the Holy Spirit.

ROMANS 15:13 GW

You give me hope. Uncle Sam can't give joy, peace, or security that lasts. Although my commanding officer thinks he runs my life, I know You are in control. I receive my joy from You, not my job or my circumstances or my training. Even though I do receive the promotion or the posting I've prayed for, it's You who gives me joy.

Because disappointments sometimes come, I might not earn the promotion points I need, or my next posting might take me away from my family. But I believe Your hand is in these circumstances. Thank You for filling me with joy; as I put my faith in You, I will overflow with joy to share with others.

Lynette Sowell

I JUST KEEP GOING AND GOING AND. . .

Those who hope in the LORD will renew their strength. They will soar on wings like eagles; they will run and not grow weary, they will walk and not be faint.

ISAIAH 40:31

Because I hope in You, You empower me to do what I can't. My body rebels during PT, 3:00 a.m. formations, or days spent in field exercises. When my body is taxed during desert training, You refresh me and I continue. Though my mind is zapped from studying for the promotion I want, You keep me alert. Though my heart aches when I'm separated from my family, You give me hope of our reunion. You energize me to be the best soldier I can for You.

As I continually hope in You, I receive the strength You pour into me. I have endurance from You, and it's more than physical or mental strength. Thank You, Lord! I couldn't do it without You.

Lynette Sowell

GOD'S R & R

Find rest, O my soul, in God above;
my hope comes from him.

PSALM 62:5

Rest? How can I rest with middle-of-the-night phone calls? Sometimes my soldiers ask much because of their personal problems. Yet I call on You in the same way, and You never tire of listening. You refresh my soul with hope, so I can give to soldiers who depend on me. Thank You for continued strength to do what I must for them and for my country.

Teach me the value of rest, especially when it's time to "hurry up and wait." Just when I thought I was shipping out, Uncle Sam changed the date again. My family never knows if I'm coming or going.

Our hope comes from You as we enjoy our time of rest together.

Lynette Sowell

SERVE WITH HONOR

*Humility and the fear of the LORD bring wealth
and honor and life.*

PROVERBS 22:4

Sometimes, Lord, I feel so pressured to put honor above everything else in life that I fail to honor You. Forgive me when I forget my priorities. I must honor those with higher rank. I must serve with honor. I know You want me to do my best to serve my country, my family, and others. But it's so easy to put duty above serving You.

Help me to remember that all honor comes from You, my Supreme Commander. I want to serve You in all that I do. I want to honor You because You are worthy. You created me, and all that I am is because of You. My wish is to honor You with the way I live my life—today and every day.

Sunni Jeffers

ADVANCEMENT

*Your beginnings will seem humble,
so prosperous will your future be.*

JOB 8:7

This life is hard, Lord. I don't mean to complain, but I see people in other jobs who seem to have it easy. They didn't have to start at the bottom and work their way up in baby steps. Sometimes it doesn't seem fair, but then I remember that You are always faithful and just.

Your Word says I can have a prosperous future, and I know You keep Your promises, Lord. Help me to become the person You want me to be, so that I will be in Your will.

I place my future in Your hands. You alone are able. I will work hard, as unto You, and trust You to take care of my future.

Sunni Jeffers

REWARDS FOR SERVICE

For whoever exalts himself will be humbled,
and whoever humbles himself will be exalted.

MATTHEW 23:12

Dear Lord, I see the bureaucracy around me, and I wonder if anyone really cares. Is being in charge all that matters?

Jesus showed us a different way. When He came to earth, He taught us to serve and be humble, just as He was a humble servant. To the world, that doesn't make sense. Jesus is the King of heaven. You exalted His name above all names. The kings and dictators of the earth fall to ruins, but You raise Your children in victory because of Your Son, Jesus.

I am Your child, Lord. Help me to be humble and to serve those above me and also those below me. Thank You for saving me and lifting me up.

Sunni Jeffers

DISCOURAGEMENT

Humble yourselves before the Lord,
and he will lift you up.

JAMES 4:10

When I see an eagle soar, I think of You, Lord. When I watch airplanes scream overhead at Mach speeds, I think of Your awesome power. I am amazed, Father, that You loved me enough to send Your Son to die for me. So many enemies surround me and temptations beckon me. The world offers pleasure, wealth, and status. But I know that without You holding everything together, the eagle would fall and the jets would crash. I want Your love and power on my side, Father.

You are the Almighty, the high and lifted up. You alone are worthy of praise. I love You, Lord. Lift me up, so I can soar like the eagle and reach up to You.

Sunni Jeffers

WALKING IN TRUTH

The man of integrity walks securely, but he who takes crooked paths will be found out.

PROVERBS 10:9

These are difficult days, Lord, and sometimes the road I travel is so hard. I am constantly faced with situations and decisions that tax me to the limit. Some days the difficulties seem almost insurmountable, and my spiritual steps seem to falter.

Sometimes it would be so much easier to take the convenient path and just be a part of all that is around me—to let circumstances and the pull of the easy way guide my steps. Thank You, precious Lord, that in those moments when the crooked paths seem to be the better paths, You touch my heart and remind me that Your way is the way of hope. . .the way of strength. . .and the way of truth.

Thomas Smith

GOOD EXAMPLE

*In everything set them an example by doing
what is good. In your teaching show integrity,
seriousness and soundness of speech that cannot
be condemned, so that those who oppose you
may be ashamed because they have nothing
bad to say about us.*

TITUS 2:7–8

Dear God, in the quiet moments the memories come. Memories of those who have been such a great part of my life. Family and friends who didn't try as much to teach me the lessons of life as they did to live them. I think back to those who reached out to me when I needed them the most, the people who were content to give to those around them with no thought of reward.

Heavenly Father, create in me such a strong sense of Your Spirit that others may see You reflected in all I do and say. Help me to be Your hands and heart in this place—not because I try to be, but because I cannot help but be.

Thank You, God, that Your love can have that much power over my life.

Thomas Smith

ENDLESS SOURCE OF HOPE

*May integrity and uprightness protect me,
because my hope is in you.*

PSALM 25:21

Sometimes I am troubled, Lord. Troubled because there are so many I meet who have lost hope or, worse, have never really had it. Their lives consist of moving along from day to day with no real sense of joy and no sense that there is something greater than all of us.

They have no place of refuge, no place from which to draw strength. They have only today, with no real thought of the future.

Thank You, Jesus, that You have banished such darkness from my life and replaced it with the healing light of Your love. I'm thankful that any thought of the future is filled with the promise of Your everlasting presence and that Your promises are the endless source of all hope.

Thomas Smith

Willingness

I know, my God, that you test the heart and are pleased with integrity. All these things have I given willingly and with honest intent. And now I have seen with joy how willingly your people who are here have given to you.

1 Chronicles 29:17

I am constantly amazed, gracious God, at how You stand ready and willing to bless me. Sometimes when I pray, I can feel that You are listening. And when I ask for Your strength, Your guidance, and Your forgiveness, I experience Your response in every part of my being.

When I am tested, and I call out to You, I know You stand ready to uphold me and bring me through whatever I may face. And in those times when I try to find my own way, Your willingness to take me back into the fold fills my heart with joy.

Thank You, dear God, that no matter how willing I am to receive Your grace and Your mercy, You are even more willing to offer it.

Thomas Smith

GIFT

The LORD has done great things for us,
and we are filled with joy.

PSALM 126:3

Lord, I'm guilty of forgetting that the good things in my life come from You. I boasted when I got a job and provided for my family when jobs were hard to find. I neglected to tell anyone You opened the door of opportunity for me.

Then, the day I enlisted in the military, a physical was required to determine my fitness to defend our county. I took credit for the good report from that, too. I bragged about how I stayed in shape by eating right and exercising my body. I didn't tell others that You gave me wisdom and an understanding of good health and what food to eat.

I want to share the joy of what You have done for me with others, and especially tell them about Your Son, Jesus Christ, the greatest gift of all.

Flavia Crowner

GLADNESS

May the nations be glad and sing for joy,
for you rule the peoples justly and guide
the nations of the earth.

PSALM 67:4

I rejoice in You, Lord, who rule all nations. You are a just God. You see what is in my heart and mind; nothing is hidden from You. In the Bible You have given me rules for living a righteous life. As one of Your children, I am to spread Your Good News throughout every nation so that others will learn about You.

We have various ways available to us to share the message that You are the King of all things under heaven and on the earth.

I pray that our president and government leaders and the leaders of all the nations of the earth will look to You for guidance.

Flavia Crowner

ENJOYMENT

*So I commend the enjoyment of life,
because nothing is better for man under the sun
than to eat and drink and be glad. Then joy will
accompany him in his work all the days of the life
God has given him under the sun.*

ECCLESIASTES 8:15

Oh, how like You it is to bless us with the enjoyment of life: food, drink, and gladness! You want us to come together to enjoy the nutrition of good food to strengthen our bodies, refreshing drinks to quench our thirst, and laughter to uplift our spirits. This merriment accompanies us throughout the days of our lives. It affects how we feel toward others. It gives us the desire to serve our country and to protect the right to pursue happiness and well-being.

Lord, I thank You for blessing me with new friends while away in the military. You made a way for me to share my personal walk with You and the promise for eternal life in Jesus Christ.

Flavia Crowner

GIVE THANKS

Be joyful always; pray continually;
give thanks in all circumstances,
for this is God's will for you in Christ Jesus.

1 THESSALONIANS 5:16–19

Dear God, while I'm away defending our right to freedom, I know You have instructed people to pray for my safety day and night, no matter what the hour. I give thanks in all circumstances concerning the reports I hear concerning the nations at war. You are in charge and already know the outcome. You have commanded us to be joyful always. I am encouraged, and I rejoice that You are watching over me. You have charged Your angels to protect me in battle, so I will be strong in You.

I'm grateful, Lord, that I have a family who will obey Your Word and pray. Thank You, and I pray that they are safe and in good health.

Flavia Crowner

A Promise Fulfilled

Follow justice and justice alone,
so that you may live and possess the land
the LORD your God is giving you.

DEUTERONOMY 16:20

Heavenly Father, sometimes it is so easy to let my emotions rule over my heart. It is easy to confuse vengeance with justice. To repay wrong with wrong. Because sometimes, dear God—just sometimes, when I get caught up in the moment and my defenses are down—I lose sight of the goal. At times, when my spirit is weary, I am tempted to take the easy way out and repay others in kind.

But in those moments You speak to my heart, and I remember. I remember what I am about. I remember that I am Your child and that Your love can overcome any obstacle that I put in the way.

Thank You, God, that You love me enough to let others see that love through me.

Thomas Smith

A Double-Edged Sword

*When justice is done, it brings joy to
the righteous but terror to evildoers.*

Proverbs 21:15

Hosanna! Glory to Your holy name, almighty and everlasting God!

Every time I see evidence of Your power in my life and in the lives of those around me, I am struck by Your infinite capacity to use us for Your glory.

Thank You, gracious God, that You have seen fit to take my life and use it. The mere mention of Your name can bring a smile in the midst of pain, and it sends the demons that would infest my life fleeing from the light of Your love. There is power in Your name!

Please, heavenly Father, use me in whatever way You will to stand with those who feel they have no advocate, to speak for those who feel they have no voice, and to stand against those who want to do them harm.

Thomas Smith

GOD'S RIGHTEOUSNESS

He will judge the world in righteousness;
he will govern the peoples with justice.

PSALM 9:8

Almighty God, I can't begin to count the number of times in my life when I have been less than You called me to be. And yet, when I realize what I have done to You and what my life has become, You pull me to Yourself and let me rest. You instill in me Your grace and the desire to be fully Yours.

I know that it is not on my word alone that You respond. Your Son paid the price for my sin, and You have accepted the sacrifice. And even more amazing is that You don't hold against me the penalty He paid on my behalf.

Instead of condemning me, You clothe me in Your righteousness and send me back into the world whole. Thank You, precious God, for all the ways You have blessed me.

Thomas Smith

LIFE WITHOUT BLINDERS

"This is what the LORD Almighty says:
'Administer true justice; show mercy
and compassion to one another.' "

ZECHARIAH 7:9

Teach me, blessed Lord, to be Your hands in this place. Help me to always remember that my way is not the only way. And please, holy Lord, never let me come to the place that I ignore the needs of others because of my own needs.

Never let me be oblivious to the suffering of those around me because of my own perceived problems. Help me to live a life of purpose, not of convenience.

You have been so good to me, and my life is rich because of Your many blessings to me. Help me always to remember that someone else may get his or her first glimpse of You through me. Gracious God, fill me with Your Holy Spirit and grant that I may live a life of service to others and devotion to You.

Thomas Smith

BEHIND THE SCENES

Moses inspected the work and saw that they had done it just as the LORD had commanded. So Moses blessed them.

EXODUS 39:43

You know, Lord, I do a lot of paperwork that never gets inspected. Much of my labor is behind the scenes. Sometimes no one knows how much or how little effort I've put into getting something done—except, of course, for You.

You know if I have given my best effort or if I've done a hurried job. I want to know, Father, that when I stand before You, You will say, "Well done."

Whatever my hands find to do, I want to do it with all my heart. Give me a willing spirit to work always for Your glory. Since You dwell within me, Lord, all I do reflects on You. I desire to mirror the greatness that is You.

Melody Lee

THE SABBATH DAY

*Observe the Sabbath day by keeping it holy,
as the LORD your God has commanded you.*

DEUTERONOMY 5:12

Sometimes I must work on the day we've set aside to worship. Then again, sometimes I could go to church, but exhaustion makes the Church of the Feather Pillow tempting. Remind me, Lord, that You have given us six days to labor and have only asked us to put aside one day for You alone.

If my schedule requires me to work, let me still find time to remember You quietly in all I do. When I want to roll over rather than join my brothers and sisters at services, remind me that my soul needs recharging, too.

You know we function best when we join with the assembly in gratitude for all You have done. Teach me what it means to keep the Sabbath holy.

Melody Lee

GIVING

Give generously to him and do so without a grudging heart; then because of this the LORD your God will bless you in all your work and in everything you put your hand to.

DEUTERONOMY 15:10

I work so hard, Lord, that sometimes I think I deserve to spend the fruit of my labor on myself. I want to keep what is mine. After all, I'm not being selfish; I have bills to pay. Besides, I deserve some fun, and I ought to have a few nice things. Right?

Okay, maybe I've forgotten that everything I have comes from You. Open my heart, dear Lord, to give—not sparingly, not grudgingly, but in true generosity. Remind me that everything I have, everything I am, comes from You. I should never look at it as giving away what is mine. I want to willingly return an offering freely out of the bounty You have given me.

Melody Lee

COMPARING MYSELF
TO OTHERS

There are different kinds of working,
but the same God works all of them in all men.

1 CORINTHIANS 12:6

Sometimes I have a tendency to see my assignments, or skills, as more important than the work of others. I start to feel proud, and I think, *Hey, look what I've done.* Then I get angry if people fail to recognize my accomplishments.

Other times, I wonder what I'm really offering. Compared to others, I don't measure up. I'll never be as smart or as fast or have the skill of the person beside me. Then I get discouraged.

Help me, Lord, not to compare myself to others. You ask only that I use the talent You gave me. If You gave me much, You expect much. If You gave me little, You expect only what I have.

Melody Lee

FOLLOWING FAITHFUL LEADERS

*Remember your leaders, who spoke the work
of God to you. Consider the outcome of their
way of life and imitate their faith.*

HEBREWS 13:7

I praise You, God, for leaders You have chosen to
do Your will. When they respond in faith, You
bless them and the people who follow their lead.
May our nation's leaders in Congress, the military,
the judiciary, and business and industry become
leaders who depend on Your Word and listen to
the voice of Your Spirit.

Lord Jesus, faithful leaders sought Your will
when they fought the fight to deliver our nation
from oppression. May our present military leaders
seek Your will as they are called to lead men and
women in combat.

Father, as I seek to follow faithful leaders, I
want to become more faithful, glorify You with
my life, and lead others to You.

Edward G. Spongberg

OBEYING THE SPIRIT

*You must act according to the decisions they give
you at the place the LORD will choose.
Be careful to do everything they direct you to do.*

DEUTERONOMY 17:10

O God of grace and power, You have called nations into being and set the standard for leadership to guide the people. Through prophets and pious believers, You have revealed Your Word to be followed. Your only Son, our Savior Jesus, became flesh and blood and lived among people. They saw His glory reflecting You, the one true God. His life revealed Your love and grace.

I pray that many will be obedient to Him as through Your Spirit You reveal the truth in Your Word. Your truth is the way to peace, but this world is full of trouble.

I praise Your name, because You have overcome the world. Help me to be obedient to You and to rejoice in my salvation.

Edward G. Spongberg

BEING ATTENTIVE TO AUTHORITY

*"Now go; I will help you speak
and will teach you what to say."*

EXODUS 4:12

Great God, when You spoke to Moses at the burning bush, You got his attention. You called him to follow You and speak for You. And he did. You made him a leader who could speak and could lead a migrant people on the march. He led well not because of his own abilities, but because he was attentive to Your voice.

In the military I learned what it means to be attentive to the orders of my superiors. May I be even more attentive as You speak through Your Word. Don't let me say, "Yes, sir!" and then do only what was spoken instead of doing all that I know was meant to be done.

Lord, I'm listening. Speak to my heart.

Edward G. Spongberg

FOLLOWING EAGERLY

*"Give me wisdom and knowledge,
that I may lead this people, for who is able
to govern this great people of yours?"*

2 CHRONICLES 1:10

Lord, help me to learn a lesson from Solomon. When he was eager to hear Your voice and do Your will, he built a temple to remind his people that You were the great architect of the nation. When in selfish eagerness he turned to glorify himself, the nation raged with civil strife.

I pray that the world leaders You have called will become eager to follow You and will turn from temptations to make themselves great.

Lord Jesus, keep me eager to follow You and faithfully witness Your power to transform life. Awaken me. When I become self-centered, hear my confessions and forgive me. I know Your blessings will come when I am eager to follow You.

Edward G. Spongberg

DAY BY DAY

Jotham grew powerful because he walked
steadfastly before the LORD his God.

2 CHRONICLES 27:6

You are my God—a God who cares about His creation. Lord, You are all-wise and all-powerful, and I put my trust in You. Teach me to walk before You with consistency and to always seek Your will in every area of my life.

I want my life to reflect Your goodness and grace to everyone I see. I want them to see what life is like with You so they will want You in their lives. Help them see that the only reason I am able to do what I do on a daily basis is because You are with me, giving me the wisdom and strength to do so.

Amy S. Huehl

PERFECT PEACE

You will keep in perfect peace him whose mind is steadfast, because he trusts in you.

ISAIAH 26:3

God, so many times You have kept me in perfect peace in the past. Be my peace now, when I need You the most.

As I dwell in Your Word, I learn to trust in You more. I find peace as I trust in Your sovereign power, knowing that whatever I face I can trust You to keep my heart in peace.

I look to You when the troubles of life overwhelm me and I want to run away. It is then—at my weakest moment—that You remind me that You are stronger than I am.

Know my thoughts, Lord, and calm them with Your presence when my life is filled with chaos.

Amy S. Huehl

YOUR WORD

*Oh, that my ways were steadfast
in obeying your decrees!*

PSALM 119:5

As I study Your Word, God, help me know what You are saying to me. Like the psalmist, I want to delight in obeying Your commandments. Help me take them into my life and to measure my life by what You have laid out for me in Your Word.

Remind me not to look to other solutions in my life for help when I need You more than anything else. Let me be quick to obey and slow to turn to things that would distract me from You.

I will seek the wisdom found in Your Word before I act in any situation. Help me live my life in a way that would honor You in all that I do.

Amy S. Huehl

IN THE MIDST OF THE PROBLEM

The God of all grace, who called you to his eternal glory in Christ, after you have suffered a little while, will himself restore you and make you strong, firm and steadfast.

1 PETER 5:10

God, I understand that for right now You have me going through this unpleasant situation. I know that once it is over and I am on the other side, I will appreciate that You have allowed me to be here for a purpose—Your purpose.

In the midst of this problem I can't see why You have me here, but I trust that You will not just get me through this but will allow me to be strong and steadfast in You. I thank You that You have allowed me to be strong up until this point.

I have faith that You have placed me here, and I will be strong in my weakness as I lean on You.

Amy S. Huehl

GIVING MY ALL

*If you faithfully obey the commands
I am giving you today. . .then I will send rain
on your land in its season. . .so that you
may gather in your grain, new wine and oil.*

DEUTERONOMY 11:12–14

Wow, God, nothing like setting the bar high for us to reach! I do not have to tell You that I have fallen short many times in keeping Your commands. Sometimes, when I seem to do them faithfully, there may be a portion of my heart that is not sold out to You.

I guess I am wondering, do I still get some of Your blessings, like the rain and seasons of the year?

I know that Your blessings are not solely based upon my obedience to You but that they come out of Your love. Father, I love You and I really do want to obey everything You have asked of me. I know that sometimes I will fail, but Your love for me will continue. I'm thankful for that.

Help me to fully yield my whole heart and soul in obeying Your will. I know that obeying You brings newness of life and blessings.

Thomas B. Webber

FOLLOWING THE LEADER

*Obey your leaders and submit to their authority.
They keep watch over you as men who must
give an account. Obey them so that their work
will be a joy, not a burden, for that would
be of no advantage to you.*

HEBREWS 13:17

Lord, it is a joy to work for leaders who love You and know the needs of their people. I would follow these leaders into the darkest battle.

However, Lord, all leaders are not created equal. Some leaders think only of themselves and forget about their troops. These leaders are hard to follow, even when we are not at war.

God, my patience is tried when I have to follow the leadership of those who care about self and not the team. Yet, You did not tell me what kind of leaders to follow—only to follow my leaders, because the result will be a benefit to my leaders and me.

Give my leaders wisdom and strength, and help me bring joy to them by faithfully following them.

Thomas B. Webber

RESIDING WITH GOD

"If you obey my commandments,
you will live in my love.
I have obeyed my Father's commandments,
and in that way I live in his love."

JOHN 15:10 GW

Not many people get to stay in Your house, Lord. If I plan to be part of Your family and reside in Your home, then I need to obey You.

Being part of a family means that I should reflect the characteristics of that family. Your family is characterized by obedience and love. If I obey You, then I must love You; and if I obey and love You, then I am part of Your family.

Show me, Lord, where I fail You with a lack of obedience and love. Walk with me every step on this journey called life, and move me ever closer to a life committed to obedience and love.

Thomas B. Webber

FAILING TO OBEY

Be careful that you do not forget the LORD your God, failing to observe his commands, his laws and his decrees that I am giving you this day.

DEUTERONOMY 8:11

Lord, You know I am not a person who can easily be told what to do. I have even been called a "self-made person." I can lead others, influence groups, and even gain victory through isolation.

I was just about to leave You out of my life when Your Spirit reminded me of some important truths: You are the One who has given me life; You have rescued me from all my enemies; You have blessed me with skills and abilities; and You have told me how to please You in all that I do and say.

Lord, never let me get so full of myself that I forget about You and the things that please You. Obeying You is better than making a name for myself.

Thomas B. Webber

EXPERIENCING FEAR

So wherever you go, make disciples of all nations.
Baptize them in the name of the Father, the Son,
and of the Holy Spirit.

MATTHEW 28:19 GW

Lord, I am in this strange land, fighting for my country. I despair as fellow soldiers die around me. I am fearful. I wonder, *Will I be next?*

Give us courage, Lord, and wisdom to face each day anew and to wear the uniform with pride as we lay down our lives for our loved ones back home. The enemy surrounds us in hate and indifference. If they only knew You, Your love would replace their hate and animosity.

Lord, if only I could do something! As Your patriot, I want Your love and peace to shine in and through me.

Birdie Etchison

SEEKING GUIDANCE

*"May nations serve you and peoples bow down
to you. Be lord over your brothers, and
may the sons of your mother bow down to you.
May those who curse you be cursed,
and those who bless you be blessed."*

GENESIS 27:29

Lord, as I seek Your Word, my heart is over-whelmed with the love that You have given me since that day long ago when I asked You into my heart. Your love fills my being. It hurts my ears to hear others curse You, but they do not know You and do not feel Your love or receive Your blessings.

As I mingle with those who do not believe, help me to continually sing Your praises and seek Your love and guidance. I want to be Your loving example of peace, joy, and love and show others how enriched my life is by Your blessings.

Birdie Etchison

MISSING FAMILY

*What other nation is so great as to have their gods
near them the way the LORD our God is near us
whenever we pray to him?*

DEUTERONOMY 4:7

Lord, as I am on this battlefield, I think of my family at home. I want to be there—to feel the touch of a loved one, to eat homemade blueberry pie, to sleep in my bed. But this is my place to be for now.

I rejoice because You are near me when I need You—wherever I am. I do need Your comforting, but I also need to remember how You suffered—for me.

Lord, help me remember the oath I took and what I am fighting for—freedom, love, my country, the unit. Fill me with courage as I say, "This, too, shall pass."

Birdie Etchison

OBEYING COMMANDS

*If you fully obey the LORD your God and carefully
follow all his commands I give you today,
the LORD your God will set you high above
all the nations on earth.*

DEUTERONOMY 28:1

Lord, obeying is difficult for me. But I think of how You have blessed me greatly and made me an instrument of good will, and I praise You.

I know our country is set above other nations, because the people of this country love You and fear You. I am Your servant, Your child, and Your patriot.

Prayer must be the foundation of my life. Without prayer, I am like them—the enemy. Lord, keep me on the straight and narrow. Make me strong and fearless.

Birdie Etchison

A POSITIVE OUTLOOK

"I've told you this so that my peace will be with you. In the world you'll have trouble. But cheer up! I have overcome the world."

JOHN 16:33 GW

It's not always easy to be cheerful when there is strife all around me. Let me cling to You and Your love, Lord, which surrounds me no matter what. Help me to find the good in every circumstance. I don't want to put on a false front or a happy face so people will see me as a fake. Instead, I want those around me to know I'm a positive person they can approach in good times and in bad.

Let me bless others with good cheer, so I can show them Your love.

Thank You for showing me how to live. Give me the strength to face each day with an optimistic attitude so I can make a positive impact on others.

Tamela Hancock Murray

CARING FOR OTHERS

Blessed are those who make peace.
They will be called God's children.

MATTHEW 5:9 GW

Lord, sometimes I feel anything but peaceful. Yet, through Your wondrous power, You show me how to be a peacemaker. When people asked You trick questions, You answered with firmness, tempered with a good dose of love.

You grant peace because You care about others, and You care about me. Help me show Your love by caring about others at all times. Help me not to be an instigator of strife but a person who stays calm, no matter what. Grant me the patience to treat others the way I want to be treated.

I am Your child, Lord.

Tamela Hancock Murray

FORGIVENESS

As holy people whom God has chosen and loved, be sympathetic, kind, humble, gentle, and patient. Put up with each other, and forgive each other if anyone has a complaint. Forgive as the Lord forgave you. Above all, be loving. This ties everything together perfectly. Also, let Christ's peace control you.

COLOSSIANS 3:12–15 GW

Living among others who are so alike yet so different can be tough, Lord. Humans are full of pride, selfishness, and other traits that lead to disputes. Even Your twelve disciples argued among themselves on occasion. You answered them in a spirit of love, not judgment. I want to follow Your example.

If I encounter strife today, help me to reach out in the spirit of love, step back, and try to imagine being the other person so I can see the opposing viewpoint. Close my mouth until I can speak words of kindness and forgiveness.

Father in heaven, thank You for Your love and understanding and for forgiving me. I want to show others Your mercy.

Tamela Hancock Murray

COURAGE

*"I will grant peace in the land, and you will lie
down and no one will make you afraid.
I will remove savage beasts from the land,
and the sword will not pass through your country."*

LEVITICUS 26:6

Lord, I know that peace can be gained only through strength. I am only one part of a larger team—a group of people working together who want nothing more than peace for our country, our families, and each other. Give me the strength and courage to do my part. Help me to obey my superiors without hesitation. I want to work with others so all of us can have peace within and without.

You faced the cross with valor. Grant that I may face my duties with bravery and conviction. I pray that my work will result in peace.

Lord, thank You for demonstrating power, honor, and love. Help me to follow Your example everywhere I go.

Tamela Hancock Murray

BEING MYSELF

Each of you must examine your own actions. Then you can be proud of your own accomplishments without comparing yourself to others.

GALATIANS 6:4 GW

Heavenly Father, please allow me to be an instrument to help others who struggle in their walk with You.

Comparing myself to them is as natural to me as breathing in the fresh air You have provided. But, when Your Spirit refreshes my soul, the struggles of others often become my own, and I find myself becoming bogged down with anxiety, stress, and sin.

Please help me to examine myself so that I can help others as we strive to become closer to You. I want to know that I am doing a good job in helping my friends and that You are proud of the person I am becoming in You.

Rhonda Gibson

THE LORD'S ARMY

*The brother in humble circumstances ought to
take pride in his high position.*

JAMES 1:9

Keep me humble, Lord, as I move up in the ranks of the military. It is hard not to become prideful with each advancement up the ladder of success. I want to soar like an eagle and shout to the world that I made it. But, Lord, I know that isn't Your will for me.

Humility is a powerful weapon in Your hands, Father. It will lead more and more men and women into the spiritual battle, and many souls will be saved.

If I want to advance in the Lord's army, I must keep myself humble in all that I do so that others will see a reflection of You. So, please, Lord, keep me humble.

Rhonda Gibson

JOYFUL HEART

I have great confidence in you;
I take great pride in you. I am greatly encouraged;
in all our troubles my joy knows no bounds.

2 CORINTHIANS 7:4

Thank You, Lord, for the joy I have in You. I have chosen this life of service that I live, but You knew what I would do before I was even born. You had confidence and pride in me when no one else did.

When my trials are heavy, I lean into Your strength. When I'm in a foreign country, I feel delight in knowing that You love and care for me. You are my light in the darkness. You are my shield when I enter battle.

Without You, I am nothing. Because of You, my life is complete. My happiness is secure in You. Thank You, Lord, for all Your many blessings and the joy in my heart.

Rhonda Gibson

A CHILD OF GOD

A voice came from heaven: "You are my Son, whom I love; with you I am well pleased."

MARK 1:11

Lord, I thank You for sending Jesus, Your Son, so I can be a child of Yours. You showed how much You love me by sending Your Son and allowing His life's blood to wash away my sin.

Father, like the potter, mold me and shape me so that when I am in the desert I will have the strength to endure temptation just as Jesus did. I want to be pleasing in Your sight. I want to live as Jesus did and be a good example to my companions and family.

It is my desire to hear the words, "You are my Son, whom I love; with you I am well pleased."

Rhonda Gibson

TESTIFY

Make it your ambition to lead a quiet life, to mind your own business and to work with your hands, just as we told you, so that your daily life may win the respect of outsiders and so that you will not be dependent on anybody.

1 THESSALONIANS 4:11–12

What carries more weight—what I say or what I do? Others need to see God's love and contentment in me. No amount of words can come close to the power of what is said by my day-to-day actions. Living my life and minding my own business is what I am to do; it is how I am to live as Christ taught.

Lord, I pray my life today will bring praise and honor to You. Let Your light shine through me. And when the opportunity comes my way, allow me to share why I live my life the way I do. Father, teach me not to boast on my own self or my accomplishments but to boast on You.

Roger D. Horne

DEVOTED TO YOU

Now we ask you, brothers, to respect those who work hard among you, who are over you in the Lord and who admonish you.

1 THESSALONIANS 5:12

Today a lot of value is placed on certain professions. Doctors, politicians, and even entertainers are given respect for the positions they have. What value do we place on those who work for the church and labor for the harvest? What's more respectable than one who devotes his life to the service of others? Do we respect those who serve in the way we should?

Lord, help me to remember those who work for Your kingdom—to lift them up in prayer and support them with a smile, a kind word, and an extra hand to help carry the load. Your Word says that the harvest is full and yet the laborers are few.

Thank You, Lord, for those who are working toward bringing in that harvest.

Roger D. Horne

GUIDE ME

Show proper respect to everyone:
Love the brotherhood of believers, fear God,
honor the king.

1 PETER 2:17

What is the Golden Rule? I am to treat others the way I want to be treated. As a Christian, if I am being Christlike, I am to live each day in a way that will be pleasing to You, Lord, by letting Your ways become mine. You walked this earth and treated each individual as important enough to die for on the cross.

Everyone is important. Did he not say that He would leave the ninety-nine to find the one sheep that was lost? Lord, I was once the one You sought to find.

Guide me to show Your love and respect for others, believers and nonbelievers alike, so that all can see You.

Roger D. Horne

UNDER AUTHORITY

*He who scorns instruction will pay for it,
but he who respects a command is rewarded.*

PROVERBS 13:13

In Matthew 8:5–9 we read about a soldier who told Jesus that he was a man under authority, having soldiers under his authority. He would tell others to do things, and they would obey. Further in the story Jesus said the man had great faith. Why? Not only was the man *in* authority, he also was a man *under* authority. It means he understood that no matter how much authority he had or the position he held, he was still under the command of another: Jesus.

Lord, help me to remember that we live under Your instruction, and give me the patience and courage to accept Your instruction so that I may become closer to You.

Roger D. Horne

THE NIGHT WATCHMAN

Therefore, I urge you, brothers, in view of God's mercy, to offer your bodies as living sacrifices, holy and pleasing to God—this is your spiritual act of worship.

ROMANS 12:1

As I stand at my post and darkness is all around, I hear the wind in the trees and the night birds call. I watch every shadow, and I hear every sound. I am reminded of the watchman who sat on the wall many years ago to sound the alarm if an intruder drew near.

But, Lord, I know You are in the darkness and in the breeze, and even the birds that call in the night are works of Your hands. As the night leans toward dawn and my body grows weary, Lord, I will present it to You as a living sacrifice, because I stand watch not only for my country but also for You.

Rhonda Gibson

MY DUTY

And do not forget to do good and to share with others, for with such sacrifices God is pleased.

HEBREWS 13:16

Lord, I hate to admit it, but sometimes I don't feel like doing good or sharing with others. At those times I miss my family and friends, especially when we are miles apart. I want to leave my responsibilities behind and return to those I hold dear to my heart. But then I remember it is my duty to obey Your Word.

Since I can't be with my family, Lord, please be with my loved ones until I can return home. Give me strength to do the best job I can and to share Your love with others.

As I do my duty for my country, I am doing it as a sacrifice unto You, knowing that You will be pleased.

Rhonda Gibson

SACRIFICES OF PRAISE

Offer right sacrifices and trust in the LORD.

PSALM 4:5

Heavenly Father, I offer You sacrifices of praise for all the many blessings You have given me. Above all, I love You, Lord, and I thank You for my family, my life, and my desire to serve You.

I am thankful that You keep us safe in times of war or peace. Because of Your grace and love, I can live my life trusting You to supply all my needs. Your Word makes that promise.

I pray that You will always be pleased with the work I attempt to accomplish on this earth. My soul desire is to praise Your name in all that I do and to trust in the knowledge that You are always present in my life.

Rhonda Gibson

Pass It On

"If you come with us, we will share with you whatever good things the LORD gives us."

NUMBERS 10:32

Like Moses, I often feel as though I am in the desert. Just when I think I'm alone and going to die spiritually, You send a guide to lead me back to the place I need to be in You. Thank You for sending Your servants to direct me in my walk through the desert sands and harsh winds.

And, Lord, teach me to pass compassion along to those I meet in this life so that they will be able to share in Your peace, hope, and love. Father, please bless those who have blessed me, and teach me to share their kindness with others. In the name of Jesus, I pray.

Rhonda Gibson

STOP AND REFLECT

*Instead, he must be hospitable, love what is good,
use good judgment, be fair and moral,
and have self-control.*

TITUS 1:8 GW

Lord, give me strength that I may show love, compassion, and judgment according to Your will with those who do not have a close walk with You.

It's my prayer that the blessings, talents, and gifts that You have bestowed on me will shine through me when dealing with others. Guide me to love what is good and shun anything that would not bring favor in Your eyes. Help me and guide me, Lord, to be fair and moral in dealing with those of this world who do not walk in Your light.

Lord, cause me to stop and reflect on You when dealing with people who do not know You. Give me control over myself in a way that will bring glory to You, to our comrades in arms, and to our nation.

James Cheesbro

SELF-CONTROLLED AND ALERT

Be self-controlled and alert. Your enemy the devil prowls around looking for someone to devour.

1 PETER 5:8

Lord, You are our divine shield and protector; be with us always. We pray that Your shield of righteousness will protect us from the evil of the world in which we live. Your Word tells us that "He who pursues righteousness and love finds life, prosperity and honor" (Proverbs 21:21).

We pray, Lord, to walk daily with You in Your favor. Cause our councils with others to be pleasing in Your sight. Lord, cause us to always be on the alert to the temptations of the devil and how cleverly they are disguised.

Give us the strength to resist the ways of the world and bring glory to Your name. May Your faithfulness deliver us from feeling lonely, weak, helpless, and cut off from other believers. In times like these, let us remember You promise to carry us in Your arms.

James Cheesbro

ARMOR OF GOD

*Be self-controlled and alert. Your enemy the devil
prowls around like a roaring lion looking for
someone to devour.*

1 PETER 5:8

The daily battles we face are difficult. Demands of time, energy, assets, and family can be overwhelming. We take comfort and strength in You, Lord.

We fight many battles in our lives. . . . Protect us with Your Word in our hearts. Arm us with the full armor of God: the belt of truth around our waist, the breastplate of righteousness, boots with the readiness that comes from the gospel of peace, the shield of faith, the helmet of salvation, and the sword of the Spirit.

As we have trained for military battle, we pray to continue to train for our spiritual battles. Allow us to grow in the knowledge of Your Word.

We belong to the day; let us be self-controlled by letting Your light shine through us. Lord, make us shine brightly so the whole world will know You are indeed Lord and Master of the universe.

James Cheesbro

SAYING NO

It teaches us to say "No" to ungodliness and worldly passions, and to live self-controlled, upright and godly lives in this present age.

TITUS 2:12

Lord, we thank You that the power to live as Christians comes from the Holy Spirit. Your death on the cross rescued us from sin, and we are free from sin's control. We thank You for the power and understanding to live according to Your will.

Temptations fill our daily lives through advertisements, entertainment, and gossip. Driving too fast, leaving work five minutes early or getting there fifteen minutes late, calling in sick when we are sick of the job but not physically ill—these are just a few of the temptations we face.

Lord, cause us to live life to the fullest—as if You were coming to take up Your believers before this day has ended. All glory and power to You, Lord of lords and King of kings.

James Cheesbro

APART

After saying good-by to each other, we went aboard the ship, and they returned home.

ACTS 21:6

I am reminded that separation during times of conflict is painful, but not because of the absence of family and friends; it is clouded by the fact that war may make that separation permanent.

Daily thoughts and fears of dying make it easy to slip into depression. Discouragement and doubt get me down. Will I ever return to those I love? Will I have changed? Will they have changed? It may never be as it was before I had to leave.

It is said that "absence makes the heart grow fonder." Somehow it is difficult to see the relevance of such words. I miss so much of what I love so dearly.

Lord, during this time of separation, allow me the personal peace I need each day. Be my comfort and consistency.

Steve Nagle

I Am with You

"I am with you and will watch over you wherever you go, and I will bring you back to this land. I will not leave you until I have done what I have promised you."

GENESIS 28:15

I remember the words in Psalm 23:4: "Even though I walk through the valley of the shadow of death, I will fear no evil, for you are with me." Thank You for Your promise to be with me and watch over me even when death stares me in the face.

When uncertainty and fear grip my heart, remind me that You are there. Thank You for Your promise to be with me when times get scary. Thank You for guiding my feet and for protecting my life.

Restore my soul. Restore my confidence in You. Give me strength. Separation from home does not mean separation from You. Be my strength. Be my comfort.

Steve Nagle

Commitments

"Leave your country and your people," God said,
"and go to the land I will show you."

I have been asked to go. I want to stay. My commitments to country will remove me from the familiar faces of family and friends. I am committed to fight for freedom, though, so help me trust You to show me each day how to cope with the pain of this separation.

You came to earth from heaven for a mission of love and sacrifice. You know what commitment is all about. You followed through with the most important task. You brought salvation to our broken world.

My task seems to pale in companson. Yet I pray not only for me but also for those I leave behind. I pray that in my commitment I will be faithful and strong. Help me fulfill what has been asked of me.

Steve Nagle

ABSENCE

"For what does he care about the family he leaves behind when his allotted months come to an end?"

JOB 21:21

Each day seems like a lifetime. Each month is like an eternity. My short-timer calendar fills slowly.

Sometimes I just dream of those little things: the smell of my wife's hair and her warm embrace, the delightful laughter of my children. Yet I am in such a faraway place. My reality is in another world. The sights and sounds and smells are so different from those I am familiar with at home.

During this time of being apart from those I love and care for, comfort me. Fill the void with Your peace. Fill me with the expectation of holding close those I love and miss so much. Allow the days and months to pass quickly. Fill me with Your love.

Steve Nagle

My Talents

Each one should use whatever gift he has received to serve others, faithfully administering God's grace in its various forms.

1 PETER 4:10

Sometimes I wonder if I have any gifts. What do I have to give, really? I see others with so much talent. There are those who are smarter, faster, and quicker to gain attention and praise. I forget You have given me two ears to listen, two eyes to see the need, two hands to give a gentle touch, two arms to pick up another's load.

Thank You, Father, for giving me exactly the talents I need to serve those You put in front of me. Put within me a word or a smile—to encourage others. Help me see their needs, Lord, and respond in a manner that will glorify You. I want to serve so that You will be praised.

Melody Lee

PART OF YOUR PLAN

There are different kinds of service,
but the same Lord.

1 CORINTHIANS 12:5

It doesn't matter whether I am a pilot or a foot soldier. In Your eyes, dear Lord, we are all the same. The talents You have provided and the tasks You have put before us are to be done for the common good.

Help me, Lord, to serve wherever You place me. Grant that I might see the service I provide as a part of Your plan for our future.

If I must run errands, let me run them with care. If I wash dishes, let each dish be thoroughly clean. If I plan strategies, let me do so prayerfully.

Help me remember You have chosen us all. Let me do my part for You.

Melody Lee

THE PRIVILEGE OF SERVICE

Serve wholeheartedly, as if you were serving the Lord, not men.

EPHESIANS 6:7

What a privilege to serve You. Oh, I know that when I think the assignment is beneath me, or I'm sent away from my family again, or the one in charge belittles my work, I tend to forget that my service is to You. I forget that in the final hour it is You to whom I must give an accounting.

It doesn't matter if my work is ever noticed or appreciated. It doesn't matter if I receive a parade or am spat upon; my goal should be to serve You. As I work, remind me that on the final day, my reward will be from You. I want to stand before You, knowing that I gave You the best I have.

Melody Lee

ALLEGIANCE

*No one serving as a soldier gets involved
in civilian affairs—he wants to please
his commanding officer.*

2 TIMOTHY 2:4

The world can be a distracting place. It is easy to get caught up in the politics or the gossip of the moment. It is easy to forget the identity of my commander and chief. You, Lord, are the one I serve. You are the One I want to please. Keep my mind focused on You.

Give me gratitude for the talents You have given me and the heart to use them. Let my work be a pleasant aroma before You. Keep me from trying to please others if it must come at the expense of doing what is right in Your eyes.

Let me always give my first allegiance to You and then to my country, family, and fellow believers.

Melody Lee

Passion and Purity

The husband should fulfill his marital duty to his wife, and likewise the wife to her husband.

1 Corinthians 7:3

Thank You, Father, for giving us the wedding gift of intimacy to bond with one another. Lord, when my spouse is with me, help me to rejoice in our union. Help me to give of myself freely and to do so with consideration and selflessness. May our physical relationship strengthen us so that when we are separated, we will not fall into temptation.

And, Lord, when we are apart, keep our minds and hearts pure for each other. Help us turn away, Lord, when we see or hear something that would tempt us away from pure thoughts. Lead us away from areas that might cause us to fall, so when we are reunited we can delight each other with passion and love.

We depend on You, Lord, for our strength.

Melody Lee

BECOMING ONE

"So they are no longer two, but one.
Therefore what God has joined together,
let man not separate."

MATTHEW 19:6

What a mystery! That two might become one. Who would have thought that marriage would be a symbol to teach us of our union with Christ? I have to admit there are times I forget we are supposed to be one. I am often selfish and want my own way. Sometimes it even appears that someone else would be better for me.

Help me trust that You have chosen the perfect mate for me, Lord. Let me remember that You have glued us together; I cannot be pulled from my spouse without being torn myself. Let me see the needs of my partner as if they were my own. Let us, as we focus on becoming one with You, become one with each other.

Melody Lee

THE GIFT

He who finds a wife finds what is good
and receives favor from the LORD.

PROVERBS 18:22

Oh, that I may always look upon my spouse as a blessing from You! May every day resonate with joy as You open our eyes to see the favor You have bestowed on us: our loved ones. Give me eyes to view Your light shining through my beloved. Give me the ears to hear of any need and the heart to respond. Grant me the gentleness to always treat my beloved as a special prize. Let me serve the one I love as I remember this was Your gift to me.

To be honest, I sometimes forget my spouse is a treasure from You. Let my first blessing always be for the one You have provided and my first thought each day to thank You for favoring me with such a gift.

Melody Lee

A PLACE OF REFUGE

*Enjoy life with your wife, whom you love,
all the days of this meaningless life that God has
given you under the sun—all your meaningless
days. For this is your lot in life and in your
toilsome labor under the sun.*

ECCLESIASTES 9:9

Let me make our home a place of safe refuge so that when the discouragement of life beats us down, we can find a place to enjoy each other. Whether at home in the States or in a foreign land, help us snuggle close to the comfort or the memory of each other.

Let me cast my burdens on You and rest in Your care so that I will not dump the world's garbage on my spouse at the end of the day.

May I find ways to bring fun into our lives and take time for dates or love notes or some token of appreciation, no matter where our work sends us or how tedious or difficult my labor might be.

Melody Lee

CONFLICT

*"You armed me with strength for battle;
you made my adversaries bow at my feet."*

2 SAMUEL 22:40

Lord, so often I depend on my courage, my intelligence, and my strength to fight and win battles. It's no wonder I fail and fall into despair. Only in Your strength can I conquer any adversary—physical or spiritual. Only *You* can bring complete victory and cause my enemies to surrender at my feet.

It seems as if the hardest battles I fight are in the war against my own sin nature. Keep my heart and my motives pure, even as I enter into conflict. Let me do or say nothing unworthy of Your servant.

Please help me to remember that You will provide the strength I need, day by day, as I trust in You.

Jill Stengl

SHELTER

The LORD is my rock, my fortress and
my deliverer; my God. . .is my shield and the horn
of my salvation, my stronghold.

PSALM 18:2

Lord, You allow me freedom to design my own offensive plan within Your clear parameters. When the crucial moment arrives and I must attack the enemy, You are my impenetrable shield. Should anything go wrong, Your communication lines are always open.

When I'm under heavy fire, I need shelter and I need it fast. Why stand in the open as a target when I can take refuge in a bombproof fortress?

Not only are You my protection, You're also the reinforcements that arrive in the nick of time to save the day. You deliver me from danger and rejoice in my salvation.

Lord, You can do it all—plan, fight, and win the battle. I stand in awe of You.

Jill Stengl

POWER

*He gives strength to the weary and increases
the power of the weak.*

ISAIAH 40:29

Lord, I want to crawl into a hole and pull the opening in after me. I'm burned out, running on empty, and sick of life. If anyone so much as speaks to me, I'll snap someone's head off. Do they think I've got more hours in my day than anyone else? That I can perform the impossible and survive without sleep?

How can my life be glorifying to You when I can't even think straight?

You promise strength to the weary and power to the weak. You brought me through today, but what about tomorrow?

You've never failed me. Never. Your promises will still hold true tomorrow.

I'll make it, Lord. *With You,* I'll make it.

Jill Stengl

WEAPONS AND MAPS

"It is God who arms me with strength and makes my way perfect."

2 SAMUEL 22:33

Okay, Lord, I'm equipped with Your strength and armed with weapons that are better than the latest breakthroughs in technological warfare. I expended my ammunition yesterday, but Your storehouse is inexhaustible. As long as I clean and "reload" every morning, by studying Your Word, I'll never hear the *click* of an empty magazine.

I can't express how thankful I am to have You keeping an eye on the big picture, far above any AWACS or GPS, organizing Your master plan. You will bring triumph out of apparent disaster, for the battle belongs to the You.

It's an honor, Lord, to serve under Your command. I will carry out Your orders to the best of my ability.

Jill Stengl

ASSIGNMENT

Whether you turn to the right or to the left,
your ears will hear a voice behind you saying,
"This is the way; walk in it."

ISAIAH 30:21

Lord, this isn't the assignment I hoped for. In short, it stinks! Was there a mix-up in Your planning department or what? I dreamed of adventure, and You gave me this hole in the wall. Why? What happened to "Ask and you shall receive"? Is there something You're not telling me?

Stupid questions, I know. I did ask You for clear direction in my life, and instructions don't get much clearer than this. I need to listen to Your voice once in a while instead of spouting off. Maybe people at this base need my fellowship; maybe I need theirs. You must have a good reason. I know You don't make mistakes.

Okay, I'm listening now. Show me the way, and I'll walk in it.

Jill Stengl

STANDBY

By day the LORD went ahead of them in a pillar of cloud to guide them on their way and by night in a pillar of fire to give them light, so that they could travel by day or night.

EXODUS 13:21

Lord, the pillar of cloud stopped. I'm tempted to blow on it a little to get it moving again. I'm ready to go whenever You say the word—whenever my orders arrive. This waiting around is getting old really fast. I want to be living for You and sharing my faith and doing my job. Anytime now would be great.

Are You listening? What? You want me to live for You while I'm waiting here? To demonstrate peace and patience and trust in Your perfect timing? Oh. I never thought of that.

Wait—the cloud is moving! My orders came. I'm out of here. Lord, forgive me for ever doubting You. Next time I promise not to blow on the cloud.

Jill Stengl

FAMILY IN REMOTE PLACES

I plan to do so when I go to Spain.
I hope to visit you while passing through and
to have you assist me on my journey there,
after I have enjoyed your company for a while.

ROMANS 15:24

Lord, You are amazing! Always, whenever I start thinking I'm the only military person who still wants to live my life for Your glory, twenty-four/seven, You supply Christian friends to encourage me and build up my faith. They're like family members spread all over the world!

I hope and pray I can help another Christian brother or sister in the same way. That's what the church is all about: helping each other grow closer to our heavenly Father and reminding each other that this earth is not our real home. We are guiding each other into God's truth.

If the military hadn't stationed me in these remote places, I would never have realized how precious my Christian family is. Thank You, Lord.

Jill Stengl

Passing Through Fire

When you pass through the waters,
I will be with you; and when you pass through
the rivers, they will not sweep over you.
When you walk through the fire, you will not
be burned; the flames will not set you ablaze.

Isaiah 43:2

I'm afraid, Lord. When I close my eyes, I still see the fiery tracers of triple-A sweeping across the black sky. Explosions rocked the earth below. Our four-ship of jets returned to base unscathed. We were thankful to be alive.

Our orders say we must fly through there again tonight. The triple-A will be even more intense. Is destroying these targets worth risking the lives of our aircrews? You brought us through safely last night, but can I expect another miracle?

Of course, I must go. I've always intended to go—and yet, my family. . .back home. . .

O Lord, protect me from this fire. I place my trust in Your promises and my future in Your hands.

Jill Stengl

WORRY

"So don't ever worry about tomorrow.
After all, tomorrow will worry about itself.
Each day has enough trouble of its own."

MATTHEW 6:34 GW

Lord, it's easy to be anxious and worried—not only for myself but also for my loved ones. I know that You are there for me, even though I can't see You. I only have to whisper Your name or think about You, and You will answer.

When You walked on the earth, a Roman soldier approached and asked You to heal his daughter. You didn't even need to go to his house to make her well. The soldier put his trust in You then. I know that You are worthy of my trust now and always.

Thank You for being steadfast and trustworthy at all times.

Tamela Hancock Murray

RELIANCE

Trust in the LORD and do good;
dwell in the land and enjoy safe pasture.

PSALM 37:3

Sometimes life doesn't seem to be either enjoyable or safe. Yet You see all, and You have a plan for me. I trust You to keep me in Your care as I watch Your plans unfold. I surrender to Your will. I give You my trust.

Peter took Your hand and walked on water. I ask that You take my hand and lead me today.

Help me to be trustworthy in every action I take so that I may show others Your love. Let everyone who knows me call me "honest" and "reliable." In that way, let me show others that You can be trusted.

Tamela Hancock Murray

Refuge

The Lord is good, a refuge in times of trouble.
He cares for those who trust in him.

Nahum 1:7

Lord, You provide for my needs each and every day, regardless of where I am or what I am doing. You give me life—a life that is to be lived in Your joy and grace, even in conflict.

Before You took the burden of the cross, You fasted in the wilderness and took refuge to pray in the Garden of Gethsemane. Likewise, I come to You for rest and refreshment. Let me take refuge in You. Fill me with Your love and grace, so that I may go back into the world and be a friend to those I encounter today. When I face trouble, remind me that You are near.

Help me to trust You. . .no matter what.

Tamela Hancock Murray

GOD'S TIMING

Trust in the LORD with all your heart and
lean not on your own understanding;
in all ways acknowledge him, and
he will make your paths straight.

PROVERBS 3:5–6

Lord, I don't always understand what's happening. I don't always see why my superiors give me certain orders. I don't always understand why my life moves too slowly sometimes, then too rapidly at other times. But I do understand that You are with me at all times. Help me to be mindful of You when I am discouraged.

For much of the time You were with them, Your disciples didn't understand some of Your actions or Your teachings. Yet everything became clear in Your timing. Help me to realize that Your timing is not always the same as mine. I pray for patience and increased understanding according to Your will.

Grant me peace as I surrender all to You without question.

Tamela Hancock Murray

BROTHERS

*How good and pleasant it is when brothers
live together in unity!*

PSALM 133:1

Brotherhood, teamwork, and united force all remind me of the importance of getting along. More than just tolerance, I pray that our relationship would grow deeper still. Unity is when two or more people are hard to separate.

Just like Your everlasting love, my heart wants desperately to find a deeper love and commitment for those with whom I live and work. Personalities are all so different. People are poor communicators. I pray that You would help me to realize the value of placing myself and my selfish ambitions aside for the sake of unity.

Those I serve with and those I live with need my commitment and support. They also need my prayers—not just for a military objective or short-term goal but that my love for You will be seen in my love for them.

Steve Nagle

ENDURANCE

May the God who gives endurance and encouragement give you a spirit of unity among yourselves as you follow Christ Jesus.

ROMANS 15:5

My faith and strength to live a holy life seem to grow weaker each day. At times I find myself wallowing in the same sins that have tripped me up so often along the way. May I turn to You for the encouragement I need just for today.

Help me realize that the endurance I need for the long haul is found only in You. I know that when I struggle with issues in my life I want to withdraw and pull away from others. I don't like the accountability that brothers in Christ demand. I am plagued with guilt and shame.

Lord, help me find forgiveness in You this hour. Help me to realize Your love. Remind me of Your sacrifice, Your pain, and Your humiliation; they paid for my transgressions.

You never condemn me. You drag me out of the "miry clay and set my feet on the rock to stay." Help me to find unity with You as I trust and obey.

Steve Nagle

LIVE IN HARMONY

*Live in harmony with one another. Do not be
proud, but be willing to associate with people
of low position. Do not be conceited.*

ROMANS 12:16

My pride gets in the way every day, or so it
seems. I feel the need to have assignments completed on time. I take pride in my work and in the
tasks I have been given to do.

Many times I find it difficult to associate with
those of lower rank or position. At times I almost
oppress those in lower ranks; it's the military way.

I pray today that I would show love to those
with whom I work and that I will not perform my
duties at the expense of others. Help me to be the
leader who is willing to lead instead of push. Remind me that a shepherd goes before the sheep.

The harmony and peace You demand of me
can never come if I have a bad attitude. Lord, I
pray that today I will develop harmony in the
workplace, at the command post, and in front of
the men and women with whom I serve.

Steve Nagle

UNDERSTANDING

Finally, all of you, live in harmony with one another; be sympathetic, love as brothers, be compassionate and humble.

1 PETER 3:8

Lord, it seems hard to remember the times when I was just starting out. Those who were looking out for my survival taught lessons I needed to learn. The drill instructors pounded into my mind and body the importance of learning those lessons well.

It took me awhile to learn the ropes, so why is it so hard for me to be tolerant of those under my care? Why is it so difficult to be encouraging to those who insist on learning lessons the hard way? I pray for tolerance for the slow learner. I pray for understanding for those who learn at a slower pace. Give me patience and grace as I remember Your patience and grace toward me.

Like the man who was forgiven the huge debt only to press his friend for the small amount owed, Lord, help me to never expect more that what I am willing to give. Create in me a clean heart, O Lord, and renew a right spirit in me. . .today!

Steve Nagle

BE STRONG

*"Be strong and let us fight bravely for
our people and the cities of our God.
The LORD will do what is good in his sight."*

2 SAMUEL 10:12

Remind me, Lord, that the battle is not for the timid but for the strong. My strength comes not from my training or my superior equipment. My source of strength comes from You.

Today I pray to receive Your strength, Your wisdom, Your courage. I know You will do what is good in Your sight.

Thank You, Lord.

Steve Nagle

GOD IS WITH YOU

"Have I not commanded you?
Be strong and courageous. Do not be terrified;
do not be discouraged, for the LORD your God
will be with you wherever you go."

JOSHUA 1:9

When the earth shakes with the sounds of war, do not let me be terrified. When the sights and sounds of war hurt my ears, do not let me be discouraged. How can I find solace in such a place?

Lord, I know You are with me wherever I go. You have commanded me to be strong and courageous. With Your help, I can be both.

Steve Nagle

CONFIDENCE

*In him and through faith in him we may
approach God with freedom and confidence.*

EPHESIANS 3:12

When I feel weak, helpless, and vulnerable, I am in awe that You are approachable, Lord. Your open arms give me freedom and confidence.

I boldly approach Your throne in faith today. May I find confidence in You today.

Help me to stand firm.

Steve Nagle

STAND GUARD

Be on your guard; stand firm in the faith;
be men of courage; be strong.

1 CORINTHIANS 16:13

When I am weak, You are strong. When I am open for attack, You give me strength. When I am afraid, You give me confidence. When my strength has given out, You give me courage.

Help me to never feel that I have let You down. I want to stand firm in the faith.

Grant me Your courage, Lord.

Steve Nagle

GRATITUDE

I thank my God every time I remember you.

PHILIPPIANS 1:3

There have been so many times, Lord, that You have blessed me with family and friends who have served our country to keep me safe from harm. When my husband was overseas, I prayed for his safe return, and You sent him home to me. His faith and Your mercy have carried us both through tumultuous times and strengthened my faith, too.

Help me, Lord, to never lose sight of what sacrifices others have made for those of us at home. Show me how to honor these men and women who perform their daily tasks in treacherous places to keep my country free.

Thank You, Lord, for bringing my veteran home and for allowing him to serve his country and You.

Veda Boyd Jones

PRAISE

His lord said unto him, Well done, thou good and faithful servant: thou hast been faithful over a few things, I will make thee ruler over many things: enter thou into the joy of thy lord.

MATTHEW 25:21 KJV

You have brought my soldier home, Lord, and You have rewarded him with Your goodness and blessings. He has served You well and has honored Your name. He has seen hard times, bad times, sad times. . .but You stood with him and helped him serve his country with courage and integrity.

Thank You, Lord, for trusting him with the burden of our times. Thank You, Lord, for giving him the strength to fight and the knowledge of forgiveness that You have brought to us all.

Thank You, Lord, for Your steadfastness that carried him through strife so that he could shout with the voice of victory. You have put Your stamp of worthiness upon him for his service for all to see.

Veda Boyd Jones

Walking with the Lord

The Lord your God has blessed you in all the work of your hands. He has watched over your journey through this vast desert.

Deuteronomy 2:7

Lord, what a journey we have had—You and I walking together! In times of need or times of plenty, You have been my strength, my stay. As I look back, those are familiar roads. Though some were rough, I know them, and I know how You sustained and guided me. But now I face new ways and new roads, and at times I have to admit that I'm scared.

Please help me to remember that, just as in the past, You will lift me up on eagle's wings; You will take hold of my hand and lead me. As I walk this new road, though tempted by distractions, I will keep my eyes fixed ahead—on You. And together we will face tomorrow.

I will continue to be strong because of Your presence within me. Thank You for always being with me.

David W. Girardin

DEDICATED SERVICE

Those who have served well gain an excellent standing and great assurance in their faith in Christ Jesus.

1 TIMOTHY 3:13

Lord, little did I know that when I joined the military You were calling me to serve in Your fields. But I did. And as the days turned to weeks and the weeks turned to months, it became more and more evident that I was not just in a job but that You had called me to serve. And serve I did—not for my sake but for what You did for and in me. You empowered me to go into new territories, places that stretched my comfort zone, but I went. At times I knew that in my own strength I would not make it; I would fall short. But through Your strength I could—and did—do it all.

Now at the end of the days, I look back and listen closely with humility. I hear Your recognition of "Well done, good and noble servant."

I pray that You will continue to strengthen me and show me more territories.

David W. Girardin

STANDING IN THE VICTORY OF CHRIST

But thanks be to God, who gives us the victory through our Lord Jesus Christ.

1 CORINTHIANS 15:57 NASB

Lord God, thank You for the ultimate victory that You guarantee us because of Christ's resurrection, by which He broke the power of death. It is good to know that, no matter what occurs here on earth, we will one day stand in Your presence and experience eternally the victory won for us.

Help me, Lord, to live my life in light of Christ's victory without fear. May my experiences and circumstances be colored and evaluated by Christ's victory. I will not fear, because Jesus rose again. Thank You for the power that Christ's victory gives me to live this day.

Jim Ellis

God's Power

O Lord, the king rejoices in your strength.
How great is his joy in the victories you give!

Psalm 21:1

Wise men know, Lord, where their strength comes from. It is not by my power or my might but by Yours that things are accomplished and circumstances are controlled. Lord, forgive me for believing that I accomplish my daily activities. Forgive me for thinking that I am in charge. Lord, help me to see that it is You working within me to bring about Your plan, in Your time, for Your glory. Be patient with Your servant, Lord. Help me to acknowledge You when the things I accomplish bring glory to me. May I testify that it is You and You alone who gives me strength to run the race; and it is You who grants success.

Jim Ellis

PREPARING FOR THE BATTLE

"For the LORD your God is the one who goes with you to fight for you against your enemies to give you victory."

DEUTERONOMY 20:4

Lord, as I stand with these pilots and aircrew before these aircraft that will soon depart to fight the enemy, we acknowledge that You go before these marines and that You go with them as they engage the enemy. Lord, thank You for the safety that You will provide. Keep these aviators vigilant as they fly in the darkness.

What is true, Lord, in the physical battle is true in the daily spiritual battles we face. Your presence goes before us and guards us in the battle for our minds. Thank You, Lord, that You fight for us and that You give us the faith to stand against our enemies. We choose today to put on the armor of God as these marines have donned their body armor so that we may be prepared to stand in the battle as You lead the way.

Jim Ellis

A VICTORIOUS PERSPECTIVE

But you give us victory over our enemies,
you put our adversaries to shame.

PSALM 44:7

I acknowledge through this prayer that there have been times when I have experienced Your power working through me to provide me victory over my enemies, and I have given You no credit, Lord. I have—in pride—fully let others believe it was my great thinking ability or planning that brought about the results. Forgive me, Lord.

Lord, forgive me also for the times I have flaunted the victory over my enemies and not been humble and contrite.

Lord, Your provision and protection are wonderful indeed. Help me to testify of Your goodness to those who don't know You and have only experienced Your care in a general way. Thank You for Your care and concern for me. Help me care about and be concerned for my enemies.

Jim Ellis

CONFLICT

*"You will hear of wars and rumors of wars.
Don't be alarmed! These things must happen,
but they don't mean that the end has come.
Nation will fight against nation and kingdom
against kingdom. There will be famines and
earthquakes in various places."*

MATTHEW 24:6–7 GW

I see our world is a place of constant strife. Having partaken in the realities of war, I am reminded firsthand of its terror. Conflict and pain transform peace. Rumors of upcoming operations upset me. Quiet my heart, O Lord. Bring peace to our world. Remind me, as in childbirth, a new beginning does not come without pain and suffering.

We pray that Your return will come quickly. I pray for those who serve in the armed forces today. May they be strong as they face many conflicts far from home.

Steve Nagle

BATTLES

*When you go to war against your enemies
and see horses and chariots and an army greater
than yours, do not be afraid of them, because
the LORD your God, who brought you up out
of Egypt, will be with you.*

DEUTERONOMY 20:1

The sights, smells, and sounds of war are with me daily. Memories of being frozen with fear rattle in the back closet. Feeling guilty for having survived haunts me. Sorrow for those lost crushes me. I cannot bear these memories alone.

As You have fought the battles in the past, fight the battles that rage in my soul today. Remind me of Your faithfulness. Remind me of Your compassion and love.

Quiet the storms in my life. Calm my fears as I am reminded that You are with me.

Steve Nagle

FEAR FACTOR

After I looked things over, I stood up and said to the nobles, the officials and the rest of the people, "Don't be afraid of them. Remember the Lord, who is great and awesome, and fight for your brothers, your sons and your daughters, your wives and your homes."

NEHEMIAH 4:14

When waves of fear wash over me, help me to stand. My hands are shaking out of control; calm my spirit. When blistering heat and blowing sand blind me, help me to see. Sweltering tropical heat saps my strength; refresh my soul. Bitter winds blow a chill to my bones; warm my heart.

When I feel drained, exhausted, and discouraged, help me to do what is asked of me; restore my soul. Give me Your strength when fear grips my heart. Remind me of Your awesome power. Let me see the bigger picture. I have been asked to protect freedom. I look to You for strength in the darkest hours. Help me to be faithful.

Steve Nagle

DEFENDER

*If ye go to war in your land against the enemy
that oppresseth you, then ye shall blow an
alarm with the trumpets; and ye shall be
remembered before the LORD your God,
and ye shall be saved from your enemies.*

NUMBERS 10:9 KJV

Conflict and oppression in our world must be met with firm resolve. I pray for those who guard the gates of freedom today. It seems like there is confrontation from all sides. I pray for those who defend democracy throughout the world. May they remember that You are the defender of truth.

You are the One who defends liberty. You are the One who restores the brokenhearted. You are the One who calms fears. You are the One who lifts oppression. You are the One who brings healing to the nations. You are the One who saves us from our enemies. You are our Defender. Thank You, Lord.

Steve Nagle

About the Contributors

Debra Sindeldecker, project editor, is a native of Ohio. She is married to Scott, who serves in the U.S. Navy. They live with their two daughters, Brittany and Erica, in Chesapeake, Virginia.

Kristin Bliss is the wife of SGT Jason G. Bliss, U.S. Army.

Roberto Miguel Cerda is a Services Technical Training Instructor and SSgt at Lackland Air Force Base, Texas.

James Cheesbro, Vietnam veteran, served in the U.S. Army's 178th Maintenance Company.

Kay Cornelius is the daughter of George Oldham, U.S. Army WWI veteran, and the wife of Don Cornelius, U.S. Army veteran, Korean Conflict.

Flavia Crowner lives in Michigan with her black lab service dog, Jenna.

Jim Ellis currently serves as a commander in the U.S. Navy Chaplain Corps.

Birdie Etchison had two children and a granddaughter presently serving in the U.S. Marines.

Rhonda Gibson is the wife of LCDR James Larry Gibson Jr.

David W. Girardin is the chaplain for the U.S. Navy Marine Aircraft Group 39.

Bettye Powell Glydewell is the wife of Jim Glydewell, a veteran of the U.S. Air Force.

Anne Greene is married to Larry, a retired U.S. Army colonel. Their son is an army captain.

Mary Ann Hayhurst's husband and daughter both serve in the U.S. Army.

Roger D. Horne has served in the U.S. Navy for more than thirteen years. He currently is the Systems Test Officer for the USS *McFaul.*

Amy S. Huehl served in the U.S. Army, where she met her husband.

Sunni Jeffers is the wife of retired CPO James Jeffers, U.S. Navy Submarine Service.

Veda Boyd Jones is the daughter of WWII and Korean veteran Raymond E. Boyd, and wife of Vietnam veteran Jimmie L. Jones.

Eileen Key is a retired schoolteacher, who resides near San Antonio's military base.

Melody Lee is the wife of Edward B. Lee, Vietnam veteran. Melody currently works at a rehabilitation hospital, where she serves veterans and others who have acquired disabilities.

Rose Allen McCauley has been married to her air force veteran husband for thirty-six years.

Tamela Hancock Murray is proud to be part of a family with a long tradition of military service, including the navy, army, and national guard. She is the wife of John Murray, who serves in the Procuring Contracting Office, Washington, D.C.

Steve Nagle served as crew chief and door gunner on helicopters in Vietnam during 1971–1972.

Wanda M. Royer is the stepmother of author Debra Sindeldecker and mother-in-law of ATC Scott K. Sindeldecker, U.S. Navy.

Thomas Smith is the son of J. Thomas Smith, veteran of the U.S. Air Force.

Lynette Sowell's family has served in four branches of the military.

Edward G. Spongberg retired after serving twenty years as chaplain in the U.S. Air Force.

Jill Stengl is the wife of a former USAF fighter pilot and the mother of a USAF Academy cadet.

Carol Umberger is married to a retired air force officer.

Thomas B. Webber serves as LCDR Chaplain in the U.S. Navy and is currently the 11th Marine Regimental Chaplain.

Beth Ziarnik's son served three years in the U.S. Navy.

OLD TESTAMENT

NEW TESTAMENT